C000201631

THE LONDON & NORTH EASTERN RAILWAY
IN FOCUS

SIR NIGEL GRESLEY
Chief Mechanical Engineer 1923-1941

EDWARD THOMPSON
Chief Mechanical Engineer 1941-1945

A. H. PEPPERCORN OBE
Chief Mechanical Engineer 1946-1949

To my wife Gloria
who knew not of my railway fanaticism for the first year of our marriage
(flying aeroplanes was a temporary No. 1 at the time)
but she has successfully coped with the problem for the last 51 years.

THE LONDON & NORTH EASTERN RAILWAY
IN FOCUS

John Crawley

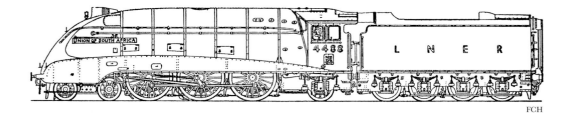

W. D. WHARTON
Wellingborough

First published in 2001 by
W. D. Wharton
37 Sheep Street
Wellingborough
Northamptonshire NN8 1BX

Copyright © John Crawley Ltd 2001

ISBN 1-899597-12-3

All rights reserved. No part of this publication may be reproduced, stored
in a retrieval system, or transmitted, in any form or by any means, electronic
or mechanical, photocopying, recording or otherwise, without
the prior permission of the publisher.

Front endpaper:
Class A4 No. 2509 *Silver Link* approaching Sandy on Saturday 1 May 1937 at the head of the up junior 'Flying Scotsman'
while K3 No. 229 sits waiting for a path through the Sandy station bottleneck. (*L. Hanson*)

Rear endpaper:
J1 No. 3003 leaving Sandy on a 'parly' on the down fast line on Saturday 1 May 1937. (*L. Hanson*)

Typeset by John Hardaker, Wollaston, Northamptonshire
Printed and bound in Great Britain by Butler & Tanner Ltd, Frome, Somerset

CONTENTS

FOREWORD

The 25-year period which saw the nation's railways being run by four companies created by the will of the government was, in many ways, quite extraordinary. It formed a kind of interregnum between wholly private-financed companies (which, with remarkably little help from government, had created the entire railway system) and the 48-year span of nationalised ownership.

Of the four big companies, the LNER has long been regarded as the least wealthy, but it was also the most imaginative. We can see, with the increasing clarity of time's perspective, that the LNER was unquestionably the railway of initiative, experimentation and advancement. The speed, comfort and appeal of its trains knocked those of the other companies into a cocked hat. And, in a way that none of the others ever achieved, the LNER had style!

With powerful locomotives sporting a truly lovely livery, many with a musical three-cylindered exhaust; streamline trains which ran faster than any others; hugely comfortable trains with a wide

Andrew Dow

variety of services on board; spine-tingling chime whistles; variety beyond the sameness of Swindon; elegance beyond anything Crewe or Derby could offer; the widespread use of the noble Gill Sans typeface and fabulous posters, it is little wonder that two or three generations of railway observers and enthusiasts were bowled over by the LNER.

One such, a youngster in the 1930s, was John Crawley. His own reaction to the LNER is to be found in these pages, and he was fortunate, when a little older, to be able to establish a growing collection of LNER items. Most numerous among them are thousands of photographs collected from official sources as well as from many friends, and this book contains a selection from the volumes which line the walls of his study. They tell a story of an imaginative company, blessed with managers who, instead of flirting with gimmickry and consultants, had the wit to leave the organisation more or less undisturbed for 25 years. Instead, they concentrated on running the best railway in the country, their minds kept in sharp focus by lack of wealth in the company coffers and mindful of the need to attract custom by more means that many would think of today.

The LNER management was responsible for 6,300 route miles of railway, 6,600 locomotives, nearly 17,000 coaches, getting on for a quarter of a million wagons, stations the length and virtually the breadth of the country, canals, hotels, docks, road motor vehicles, horses, about 200 million passengers every year, and nearly 200,000 staff.

Of course it could be argued that this was too much for one management. Indeed, in due course, when British Railways was created, the LNER was divided among three regions. Perhaps government was belatedly accepting that what they created in the 1921 Railways Act was unmanageably large. But in 1923, railwaymen had seized their new opportunity, and in a very short time had created a company that is still being talked about, celebrated and written about, over 50 years after it has gone.

Here is John Crawley's contribution to the many books that have been written about the LNER, from someone who was smitten in the 1920s and has been in love ever since.

Andrew Dow

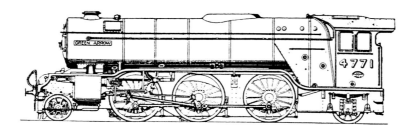

ACKNOWLEDGEMENTS

To Andrew Dow for so kindly writing the foreword to this book, and to Andrew's father George who I had the pleasure of meeting on several occasions (he joined the LNER in 1927 and rose to become their Press Relations Officer).

To Leslie Hanson for allowing me to use any of his photographs that I have in my collection.

To Dieter Hopkin, Head of Library and Archive, Philip Atkins B.Sc. and Richard Gibbon B.Sc. (Eng.), C.Eng., M.I.Mech.E., all of the National Railway Museum, who have assisted me from time to time with queries which I have raised. I also acknowledge the National Railway Museum for approving my inclusion in the book of many of my LNER Company photographs for which they have the negatives. Under each of these appears the negative number (e.g. DON XX/XX) so that readers wishing to acquire prints can do so by applying to the museum at Leeman Road, York, YO26 4XJ, quoting the relevant figure and negative numbers and also mentioning the title of this book. I must point out, however, that none of these photographs came to me via the NRM and it is possible that some of the negatives did not survive to join the national collection.

To Paul Wilkinson of HM Railway Inspectorate for permission to reproduce the King's Cross and Whiske Moor accident reports.

To the late Francis Charles Hambleton, whose company I enjoyed on many occasions when visiting him at his home in Dulwich, for his kind permission to use any of his line drawings which since his death are in the Stephenson Locomotive Society's archives.

To David King for redrawing my Doncaster chimney drawings to scale omitting the petticoats to enable them to fit within the confines of the page size.

To Anne Benham for assisting me with the more laborious tasks and to those unknown photographers whose photographs I have used without being able to acknowledge their source.

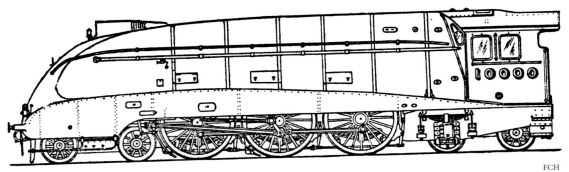

FCH

LNER No. 10000 in final form.

INTRODUCTION

This book is about a railway company that became history upon nationalisation in 1948. It is illustrated by a selection of photographs and other items of interest from my own collection, and it records some of the locomotives, rolling stock and other equipment that helped make up the London & North Eastern Railway.

My own interest in railways started on my second birthday when I was given a Hornby 0-4-0 tender engine – yes in LNER green. Since that day many more miniatures have come my way and continue to do so.

In the thirties it was my family's habit to go for a car ride on a Sunday afternoon, usually finishing up at the Everton level crossing just north of Sandy. This was an ideal spot for seeing the trains. On one side of the four-track level crossing was a cast-iron footbridge, whilst on the other side was a signal box. Once on the footbridge you could see a considerable distance in both directions as well as having a bird's-eye view of what was going on in the signal box.

The single 'ding' of a bell was the prelude to an approaching train still some miles away (the bell code at that time meant nothing to me at my young age). Then the frenzied turning of a large wheel (rather like a giant version of an old-fashioned mangle) and the four gates started to close, clicking as they overrode the gate locks set in the ground. The thump of levers being pulled over, the swish of signal wires and the movement of arms on one or other of the bracket signals located on each side of the level crossing told all – indicating up or down, fast or slow road. Then the quiet of the afternoon would return except for the noise of the startled pheasants and the still wheeling skylarks overhead.

A down train having been signalled, my eyes would be glued in the direction of the far distant Sandy station until I saw a smudge of smoke. Some minutes later the unmistakable exhaust of a Gresley engine would become audible. At that age I did not know why it was different, only that nothing on the LMS in my home town of Bedford ever sounded like it.

Excitement would grow with the ever-increasing noise of its approach until a gleaming green engine with a train of white-roofed teak coaches, with white wheel rims, would hurtle past with a roar followed by the click-click-click of the wheels receding into the distance, and that wonderful smell that only steam

John Crawley

engines know how to make left hanging in the air to convince me that what I had just seen was for real and not the figment of a vivid imagination.

Sometimes my frantic waving from the footbridge would prompt a prolonged blast on the whistle and a nonchalant acknowledgment from the driver by way of half lifting the arm he was leaning on.

My first visit to Everton, which must have been circa 1930, marked the beginning of a love affair with the LNER which continues to this day.

On my birthday in November 1935 my father had business in Regent Street in London, and my mother and I were taken with him. Whilst he was at his meeting I was taken to Hamley's, the world-famous toy shop nearby, and yet another addition was made to my 'O' gauge LNER model railway. After a quick lunch we were away again. After a while we arrived at King's Cross, somewhere I had always wanted to visit.

Parking the car was simple – you stopped at the kerbside and that was it. Leaving my mother in the car, father took me into the station where, spotting a train in the departure platform (No. 10), I wanted to see which engine was on the front but he insisted that we went his way (he had obviously done his homework) and so we walked to the end of a platform where we looked around at the activity that was taking place. Suddenly there was a whistle unlike anything else I had ever heard and there appeared from the gloom of the tunnel (Gas Works tunnel, as I was to discover years later) what I can only describe as a ghost-like silver engine and coaches which glided slowly past us and down the full length of the platform. This was none other than No. 2509 *Silver Link*.

I had, of course, read about this engine in *The Railway Magazine* but this did not prepare me for the tremendous impression it made on me. We walked down the platform amidst the alighting passengers until we reached the engine, where I stood admiring her. The cab door opened and the fireman alighted to uncouple and rearrange the lamps. The driver, who was leaning out of his cab window, noticed my admiration of his engine and said: 'Sonny, would you like to come up?' I did not need to be asked twice and with a stammered 'Yes please' I climbed aboard. The driver was kindness itself, explaining everything to me – most of which was over my head.

One thing I do remember was a matchstick stuck in the speed recorder. The recorder was located beneath the fireman's seat so that it was easily visible to the driver. When I asked what the matchstick was for, it was hastily removed. Years later I was told that you could peg the speed so that it did not show the true maximum attained. Admittedly, I have not seen it since, but I now understand there were five different speed recorders fitted to A4s in their lifetime.

After about ten minutes the driver asked me, whilst looking at my father standing on the platform, if I would like to ride down to the end of the platform. Seeing my father give a nod of approval, I said 'Yes please' once again and my first ever footplate ride began. From that point on I was truly infected by the steam bug. I am still able to re-live the thrill of that day.

In the summer of 1937 I was old enough to cycle over to Sandy for a day on the station – sometimes as many as three times a week in the school holidays. On one such occasion I had a new bicycle and being rather loath to leave it against the station wall I went into the goods yard to the little hut by the weighbridge. I asked the man if I could leave my bicycle by his hut and if he would be kind enough to keep an eye on it for me. 'Of course,' he said, and asked me if I would like a cup of tea. Inside his domain was a large and blackened kettle which stood by the fire as an ever-ready source of hot water, for he seemed to provide tea for the porters, shunters and anyone else wanting a hot drink. This became a regular routine and Mr Smith, as I came to know him, asked one day if I would like to get up on the shunter. I said that I would, and soon found myself walking with him down between the sidings to where stood a Class O1 2-8-0 which, I learnt, came down from New England each day to shunt the yard.

From now on nearly every visit included an hour or two shunting. Sometimes it would be an O2 2-8-0 – the three-cylinder engine – and on one visit the driver said: 'This day next week I shall have a pony as this old girl is due for a wash out.' The fireman explained to me that this was the nickname given to the old Great Northern 4-4-0s. As I had never seen one of this Class, I made sure that I did not miss the invitation.

The main object of the shunting was to collect together the vans from the different sidings which farmers had been loading with their produce, mainly salad stuff during the summer and Brussels sprouts, potatoes and cauliflowers in the winter. This also entailed a trip over to the North West, as the adjacent LMS sidings were still known.

This to me was exciting as it involved leaving the yard and crossing over the main lines and into the interchange siding where one or two vans from down the line towards Cambridge were waiting to be collected. These would be brought to join the other vans we had assembled and would then be placed in the down loop line at the side of the yard. After this I would climb down from the engine, bid the crew my thanks, and they would be away light engine on the slow road to New England.

Later on I would position myself on the foot-bridge at the south end of the station and await the arrival of the 3.40 p.m. 'Green Arrow' service, or 'Scotch Goods' as she was known to the railwaymen. This train usually had No. 4771 *Green Arrow* on the front, the first of her class and so named to operate the 'Green Arrow' express goods service. The vegetables that had been loaded that day at Sandy would be on sale in the Edinburgh fruit and vegetable markets the next morning.

First a shunter with his uncoupling pole would take up his position and in a few moments the *Green Arrow* would come coasting in, stopping where the shunter quickly uncoupled her from the train. A pop on the whistle and she moved forward just into the station, a whistle for the points, the shunt signal turning to 'go' and she would back down on to the waiting vans which would vary from four to nine in number.

A quick couple-up by the shunter, another pop on the whistle and she would go forward, this time a lot further down the platform. A whistle for the points, a wave by the shunter to tell the driver they had changed and back down to join his waiting train on the down fast line. Again a quick couple-up, 'Right away mate' from the shunter, a whistle and she was away fast line to Peterborough where 4771 would come off and be replaced by another V2 or a K3, which was booked. This operation took place five days a week and the smart way in which it was carried out always impressed me.

Another thing that I noticed was that some drivers wore a flat cap, sometimes with a muffler around their neck, in place of the shiny-topped black cap. These tended to be on the Pacifics and I have often wondered whether these drivers were Yorkshiremen as they were invariably on the long distance trains. This was a form of headgear that I had not seen on the LMS at Bedford. It all added character to the line.

I soon discovered that I could afford to take the train home from Sandy. From memory I think the fare was 7d, and 4d for the eight mile or so journey to Bedford with my bicycle travelling in the Guards Van.

I soon yearned to travel on the LNER so I devised a pleasant way of doing this. I would catch a train from Bedford St John's (or Bedford North West as it was known by the men) to Sandy. On one occasion, while I was looking at the engine, a Prince of Wales No. 25648 *Queen of the Belgians*, the driver, seeing my interest in his engine, invited me to 'jump up'. After a few minutes had gone by he asked me if I was travelling on the train? When I said I was, he said

'Stand over there – you'll be all right, but you will have to get into the train at Blunham (the last station before Sandy) as you never know who will be about at Sandy.'

Having surrendered my single ticket at Sandy, I then bought a Third-class single to Hitchin. This train would be the Parly, so called after the Act of Parliament passed in 1844 compelling any railway company that derived a third or more of its income from passenger traffic to run at least one train each day in each direction calling at all stations.

It amazes me that after the last war in the late forties this name still survived and may still be in use as far as I know. It was always a thrill waiting for this train as you never knew which class of engine would be on the front. Usually it would be a small Atlantic but a large Atlantic would sometimes appear, as would a green or blue Pacific.

One ride down to Hitchin was behind an A4 on a running-in turn, presumably from New England, with just an articulated twin set. Unfortunately, time dims the memory and I am unable to recall which engine it was.

Upon arrival at Hitchin I would take up my position at the south end of the up platform where it was possible to look over a low wall into the engine yard where the preparation and disposal of engines was carried out. Hitchin was also a good place to observe the fast trains which came through the middle of the station where only the two outside slow roads had platforms.

One Saturday I made a return trip from Hitchin to Hertford on Sentinel railcar *Royal Forester*. On the outward run we had a van hooked on which was left at Hertford. The riding of the railcar was not smooth. It had a slight surging movement and was definitely under-powered in my inexperienced opinion. When observing from the platform, their exhaust was more of a 'Hof-Hof' and was quite distinctive.

Around five o'clock in the afternoon it was time to go home. After passing under the station subway I made my way to the north end of the down slow road where alongside was a short bay in which would be waiting Johnson 0-4-4 tank engine, usually No. 1272, at the rear of a two coach motor set. Getting into the compartment nearest to the front of the train enabled me to travel with the window down and my head out. With the engine at the rear there were no smuts, only flies, to contend with.

At that age I found it very exciting to plunge into the 882-yard-long tunnel at Warden which had been built to accommodate double track. The stations all had two platforms but most only had single track, one platform serving no useful purpose.

Bedford was duly reached and then the only snag of the day – my bicycle had been left at St John's station which now meant a good walk from the Midland station to where I had returned.

Having taken sandwiches in my pocket, all this had been accomplished for a pocket money outlay of around 2/6d (12½p) plus the return fare to Hertford (which was a one off and I cannot recall the cost.)

I cannot attempt to guess at the number of days that I spent at Sandy during my youth. It was always a family joke that I grew up at Sandy. Be that as it may, I think I was lucky as I can recall the *Cock o' the North* coming through, the two Booster 2-8-2 Class P1s, Silver A4s (all four of them), green ones and, of course, the blue ones.

I was never a collector of engine numbers but the only two types of Gresley engines, other than shunting tank engines, that eluded me were the J38 0-6-0s and the 4-4-0 Shires and Hunts. It was 1942 in Scotland before I caught up with them.

I do hope that these memories have been of interest and have helped to form a picture in the minds of my readers. These days I wonder how many, if any, schoolboys talk railways at school. In my day most of my compatriots would talk railways – some on the fringe while others, like myself, were near fanatics.

On one occasion I recollect spending two hours on a Saturday afternoon in detention, along with my antagonist, for upholding the honour of the LNER against the stupid boy who had insisted that the GWR ruled supreme.

Unfortunately, today's youngsters are wedded to the computer and its associated games, which is a great pity for in 60 years' time it's quite likely there will be no devoted amateurs to put down their personal recollections. And the railways have lost so much of their character and characters.

In this book I have specially selected a diversity of photographs and other items with the aim of showing the LNER in its heyday to those enthusiasts not lucky enough to have seen it for themselves. As well as locomotives I have included rolling stock (both passenger and goods), horse-drawn and motor delivery vehicles, water softening plants, coaling plants and many other things which go to make a railway. All the pictures are reproduced sufficiently large to enable detail to be seen, and in this, and the inclusion of the official Doncaster drawings of the different chimneys fitted to the company's engines, I have the modeller in mind.

If any reader would like to learn more, there are two specialist societies which would welcome them as members. They are the LNER Study Group (Honorary Membership Secretary, Mr K. Tong, 18 Gray Fallow, Broadmeadows, South Normanton, Derbyshire DE55 3BQ) and the Gresley Society (Honorary Membership Secretary, Mr R. A. Wood, 6 Church Road, Twinstead, Sudbury, Suffolk CO10 7NA).

John Crawley
Bedford, 2001

LOCOMOTIVES

FIG. 1   HOPKINS-BROWN/JOHN CRAWLEY

A1 No. 1472, Works No. 1564, built in February 1923 and allocated to Doncaster shed. This photograph, taken in the Plant yard on Saturday 21 April 1923, shows well her GN loading gauge, tall chimney, high cab and without the cut-off corners at the lower ends of her front buffer beam. She received her nameplates *Flying Scotsman* and her LNER No. 4472 in 1924 whilst being prepared for display in the British Empire Exhibition at Wembley. She was withdrawn as BR No. 60103 in January 1963 and purchased privately for preservation.

FIG. 2   DON 24/9

No. 4472 under her protective dust covers standing in the Plant yard on Saturday 1 March 1924, prior to her departure for Wembley for display at the British Empire Exhibition. The connecting rods have been removed and the valve gear disconnected, whilst all steelwork has been polished.

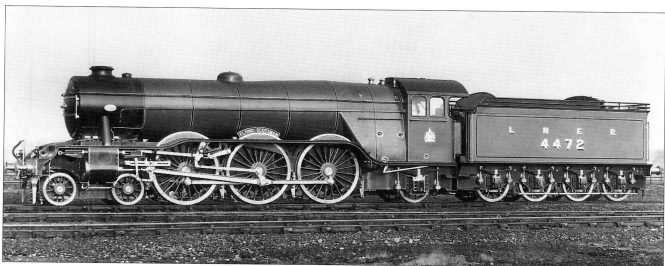

FIG. 3

DON 24/57

No. 4472 at the Plant on Saturday 29 November 1924 after returning from the Wembley Exhibition. The following year she went back to the exhibition, but this time accompanied by a six-wheeled tender (borrowed from a K3) because of a shortage of display space resulting from a revised layout. The company coat of arms was hand-painted on the cab sides – unlike so many of the companies, the new LNER never had transfers made – and she carried these until 1928 when they were removed to allow the engine number to appear on the cab sides and so facilitate the exchange of tenders.

FIG. 4

DON 30/89

No. 4472 with corridor tender at the Plant after having undergone a general repair. Photographed on Friday 14 March 1930, the day before she was released back into traffic.

FIG. 5   L. HANSON

A1 No. 4472 *Flying Scotsman* (by now a King's Cross engine) clearing Sandy station with a down fast train on Saturday 1 May 1937, having lost her corridor tender the year before and is here coupled to a Great Northern coal rail tender. The Sandy bottleneck is very apparent in this view. The tracks in the background are those of the LMS (ex LNWR) Oxford to Cambridge line.

FIG. 6   L. HANSON

A1 No. 4475 *Flying Fox*, Works No. 1567, built in April 1923 and allocated to King's Cross. Photographed at New England on Saturday 16 June 1935 whilst taking on coal, after which she will turn on the triangle (New England not having a turntable) before working back to King's Cross. She was withdrawn as BR No. 60106 in December 1964.

FIG. 7

DON 23/36

A1 No. 1479 as yet unnamed, Works No. 1571, built in July 1923 and allocated to Grantham. In September 1923 a scheme was evolved to help differentiate between engines carrying identical numbers as a result of amalgamation. A small letter was to follow the engine number and in the case of Doncaster-built engines this was the letter 'N'. Other works within the new company were also allocated their own letters. This was not the answer to the problem and the scheme was abandoned after six months. In April 1925 No. 1479's number was changed to 4479 (all ex-GNR engines having 3000 added to their numbers), followed a month later with the fitting of her nameplates – *Robert the Devil*. A story about this engine which I read somewhere many years ago has remained in my memory to my amusement. One day a special train was booked from the Cross to convey high-ranking church dignitaries to an ecclesiastical conference somewhere up north, probably York. Top Shed took great pains to clean her and to see that she was rostered for this train. Someone with a sense of humour thought it would be fun for the bishops to be taken north by the Devil. True or not, and it probably is, it makes a good tale. This photograph was taken on Saturday 14 July 1923. She was withdrawn as BR No. 60110 in May 1963.

FIG. 8

DON 27/107

A3 No. 4480 *Enterprise*, Works No. 1572, built in August 1923 and allocated to Grantham. In July 1927 she was the first A1 to be converted to Class A3 by the fitting of the 220psi boiler in place of the 180psi fitted to all A1s. The square pockets on the side of the smoke box which houses the larger super-heater header are a distinguishing feature of the A3 class. Photographed just out of shops after conversion on Thursday, 21 July 1927. She was withdrawn as BR No. 60111 in December 1962.

FIG. 9

DON 28/171

A3 No. 2544 *Lemberg*, Works No. 1600, built in July 1924 and allocated to Doncaster shed where she was to remain until January 1937. Originally built as Class A1, she went into the Plant for rebuilding to Class A3 in September 1927. Like the majority of her sisters, she carried the name of a racehorse, in this case the winner of the Derby in 1910. Photographed on Sunday 4 November 1928. She was withdrawn as BR No. 60045 in November 1964.

FIG. 10

L. HANSON

A1 No. 2564 *Knight of Thistle*, built by The North British Locomotive Company, Works No. 23102, in July 1924 and allocated to Haymarket where this photograph was taken on Sunday 1 August 1937, although by this time the locomotive had been reallocated to Eastfield. With the drain taps open and the fire thrown out, she has been coaled up ready for the next day's work. By the time the engine gets steam, the excess coal on the tender will have been used, bringing the level to within the loading gauge. She was withdrawn as BR No. 60065 in June 1964.

FIG. 11

AUTHOR'S COLLECTION

A1 No. 2554 *Woolwinder*, Works No. 1610, built in December 1924 and allocated to Doncaster shed. This photograph was taken in the summer of 1927 on a down fast train at Potters Bar, by which time she had been reallocated to Grantham. She was withdrawn as BR No. 60055 in September 1961.

FIG. 12

AUTHOR'S COLLECTION

A1 No. 2563 *William Whitelaw*, built by The North British Locomotive Company, Works No. 23101, in August 1924 and allocated to Haymarket. In July 1941 the locomotive was renamed *Tagalie* as the original name was required for fitting to A4 No. 4462. This photograph was taken at the works when No. 2563 was new, and shows her in photographic grey paint. With the amalgamation, engines travelled outside their original company's tracks, and the Pacifics, being out of gauge for the old North Eastern Railway, were found to be lifting the edging stones of platforms 8 and 10 at Newcastle Central. Hence the cut-outs on the bottom corners of her front buffer beam. She was withdrawn as BR No. 60064 in September 1961.

FIG. 13   AUTHOR'S COLLECTION

A3 No. 2580 *Shotover*, built by The North British Locomotive Company, Works No. 23118, in November 1924 and allocated to Heaton. A posed photograph taken on the turntable at King's Cross, presumably in 1928 when corridor tenders were introduced for working the 10 o'clock non-stop 'Flying Scotsman'. She was withdrawn as BR No. 60081 in October 1962.

FIG. 14   DON 28/61

The frames of an eight-wheel corridor tender under construction at the Plant on Thursday 10 May 1928.

FIG. 15   DON 28/69

Corridor tender No. 5329 outside the Plant on Tuesday 15 May 1928. Ten of these tenders were built for the introduction of the non-stop service between King's Cross and Edinburgh which began on Tuesday 1 May 1928. This made it possible for the relief driver and fireman who had been travelling in the first coach in a reserved compartment to change places with the crew who had worked the first half of the journey. Publicity would appear to be the motivation behind this venture as there was no time-saving for the travelling public. It was no quicker than the second portion of the train which closely followed it and was booked to stop at Grantham, York, Newcastle and Berwick. Both trains were timed to cover the journey in 8¼ hours. The publicity gained by the company was enormous and is still with us today. The 5th edition of *The Concise Oxford Dictionary* includes the following entry under 'Scotch': '*Flying Scotsman*, a London to Edinburgh express.'

FIG. 16.   DON 31/194

A1 No. 4473 *Solario*, Works No. 1565, built in March 1923 and allocated to Doncaster shed. This photograph, taken in December 1931, shows her undergoing comparative smoke trials with a normal smoke box near Carlton. She was withdrawn as BR No. 60104 in December 1959.

Smoke drifting down and along the boilers of steam locomotives had always presented a problem to their drivers.

In his report on the accident at Leighton Buzzard on the LMS railway in March 1931, the Inspecting Officer, Lt.-Col. A. H. L. Mount, concludes his report by saying:

... accentuates the liability for steam and smoke to drift along the top of the boiler, particularly when working lightly. This feature is noticeable on this class of engine (i.e. 'Royal Scots') and it is recognized and has been considered by the company's officers, but improvement, I understand, has not yet passed beyond the state of experiment with various forms of baffle plates around the chimney.

The Chief Mechanical Engineer informed me that wind tunnel experiments with a model are being undertaken such as those which apparently resulted in the successful design of engine No. 10,000 on the London & North Eastern Railway.

This report, no doubt, convinced Gresley that the time had come to find a cure for the problem. The first experiment involved No. 2747 *Coronach* in which the upper part of her smoke box was partitioned off and left open as an air intake, the resulting air flow exhausting behind the chimney in an upward direction and, it was hoped, lifting the smoke and steam from the chimney with it. A number of trial runs were made during October, November and December 1931, but were not considered successful and the modifications were removed in February 1933.

FIG. 17 (ABOVE) · DON 31/175

A3 No. 2747 *Coronach*, Works No. 1703, built in December 1928 and allocated to Doncaster shed. She was photographed at the Plant on Tuesday 13 October 1931 fitted with a modified smoke-lifting device. She was withdrawn as BR No. 60093 in April 1962.

FIG. 18 (BELOW) · DON 31/180

Coronach showing the exhaust orifice behind the chimney.

FIG. 19

Coronach undergoing trials with smoke-lifting smoke box near Carlton in December 1931.

FIG. 20

Coronach during smoke-lifting trials near Grantham in December 1931. The special equipment was removed in February 1933.

A3 No. 2751 *Humorist*, Works No. 1709, built in April 1929 and allocated to Doncaster shed, was fitted with a smoke-lifting smoke box which was divided in a similar manner to that fitted to *Coronach*. However, with this design the air flow entered the open top half of the smoke box and then exhausted through the rear half of the double chimney.

This arrangement was even less effective than that fitted to *Coronach* and was removed in 1933. She was withdrawn as BR No. 60097 in August 1963.

All engines are 'she' and one must wonder how poor *Humorist* must have felt continually having her good looks mutilated in the search for a successful smoke-lifting device. One of the descriptions given for the word 'Humorist' in *The Concise Oxford Dictionary* is 'a humorous actor'. She certainly came on stage enough times with many a change of costume.

Drivers always claimed that each engine had its own personality. I wonder if she still lived up to her name by the time the trials had been concluded.

These photographs show her fitted with a variety of different smoke-lifting devices. The final arrangement was said to be successful, but this must remain conjecture as no other engines were so fitted despite all the time and money spent on the experiments.

FIG. 21   DON 32/70

Humorist showing rear view of smoke-lifting chimney. Photographed at the Plant on Wednesday 20 April 1932.

FIG. 22   L. HANSON

Coronach with normal chimney and smoke box heading a down Pullman train having just passed through Sandy station on Saturday 1 May 1937.

FIG. 23

DON 32/64

Humorist fitted with the smoke-lifting double chimney. Photographed at the Plant on Wednesday, 20 April 1932.

FIG. 24

DON 32/105

Humorist fitted with new pattern smoke-lifting single chimney. Photographed at the Plant on Saturday 5 November 1932.

FIG. 25
DON 33/25

Humorist, with single chimney, fitted with side plate smoke-lifter. Photographed at the Plant on Thursday 30 March 1933.

FIG. 26
DON 38/24

Humorist fitted with double chimney and smoke-lifting side wings. Photographed at the Plant in February 1938.

FIG. 27

DON 39/84

A1 No. 2547 *Doncaster*, Works No. 1603, built in August 1924 and allocated to Grantham. This photograph was taken in June 1939 and it is recorded that she was fitted with three steel arch tubes. She was withdrawn as BR No. 60048 in September 1963.

FIG. 28

L. HANSON

A1 No. 2574 *St Frusquin*, Works No. 23112, built by The North British Locomotive Company in October 1924 and allocated to Gateshead. This photograph was taken on Thursday 4 August 1938 as she passed through Princes Street Gardens on her way into Edinburgh Waverley with a train of Pullman cars. She was withdrawn as BR No. 60075 in January 1964.

FIG. 29   DON 26/90

A1 No. 2553 *Prince of Wales*, Works No. 1609, built in December 1924 and allocated to Gorton. When she first emerged from the Plant she carried the name *Manna*. Early in November 1926 His Royal Highness The Prince of Wales paid an official visit to the Plant, during which time he inspected No. 2553 which had been renamed *Prince of Wales* in honour of the occasion. This photograph was taken on Thursday 11 November to show the new nameplates. She was withdrawn as BR No. 60054 in June 1964.

FIG. 30   DON 25/77

A1 No. 2555 *Centenary*, Works No. 1611, built in February 1925 and allocated to Doncaster shed. Photographed on Saturday 17 October 1925, although it is not recorded why she was back at the Plant at that time. Some two years later she was to emerge from the Plant as the first engine to be fitted with long travel valves which were to transform her performance, and ultimately that of her sisters. She was withdrawn as BR No. 60056 in May 1963.

FIG. 31   DON 29/74

A1 No. 2562 *Isinglass*, Works No. 1618, built in July 1925 and allocated to Doncaster shed. This photograph was taken for the Chief Mechanical Engineer's records on Thursday 16 May 1929 to show her fitted with the 'ML' type super-heater and twin anti-vacuum relief valves behind the chimney. She was withdrawn as BR No. 60063 in June 1964.

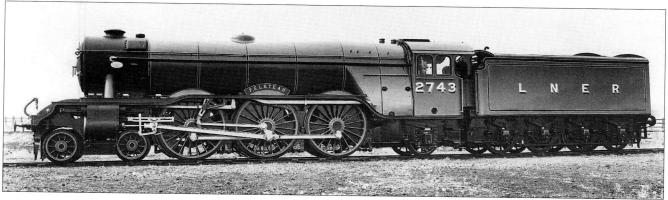

FIG. 32

DON 28/94

A3 No. 2743 *Felstead*, Works No. 1693, built in August 1928 and allocated to Doncaster shed. She was the first production A3 to be built, all previous Class A3s having been converted from Class A1s. Coupled with a corridor tender (with spoked wheels) and photographed at the Plant on Thursday 26 July 1928. She was withdrawn as BR No. 60089 in October 1963.

FIG. 33

AUTHOR'S COLLECTION

The 1928 Christmas card sent out by Robert A. Thom & Staff, Chief Mechanical Engineer's Department. The picture on this card was taken from the photograph in Figure 32 above.

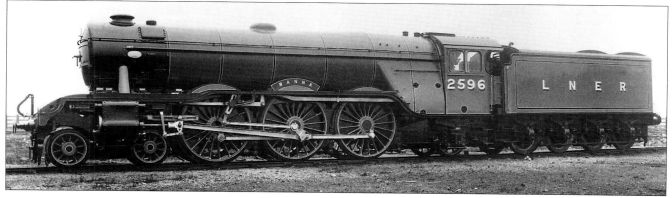

FIG. 34

DON 30/82

A3 No. 2596 *Manna*, Works No. 1733, built in February 1930 and allocated to Gateshead. She was named after the winner of the 1925 Derby and 2000 Guineas. Photographed on Wednesday 5 March 1930. She was withdrawn as BR No. 60085 in October 1964.

FIG. 35   L. HANSON

A3 No. 2597 *Gainsborough*, Works No. 1736, built in April 1930 and allocated to Gateshead. Seen here on a down express on Saturday 27 June 1936 after passing through Sandy station. She was withdrawn as BR No. 60086 in November 1963.

FIG. 36   L. HANSON

A3 No. 2795 *Call Boy*, Works No. 1738, built in April 1930 and allocated to Haymarket. On Tuesday 6 August 1935 she is shown crossing the viaduct over the River Aln on the up 'Flying Scotsman' still with a non-stop journey of 302 miles in front of her. She was withdrawn as BR No. 60099 in October 1963.

FIG. 37   L. HANSON

A3 No. 2500 *Windsor Lad*, Works No. 1790, built in July 1934 and allocated to Haymarket, and is seen there on the turntable on Thursday 4 August 1938. She was withdrawn as BR No. 60035 in September 1961.

FIG. 38   L. HANSON

A3 No. 2507 *Singapore*, Works No. 1798, built in December 1934 and allocated to Gateshead where she spent her LNER life apart from some eight months when she was sent to Neville Hill at Leeds. Caught by the camera on shed at Haymarket on Thursday 4 August 1938. She was the penultimate member of her class of 79 engines, and was withdrawn as BR No. 60042 in July 1964.

FIG. 39   DON 45/182

A1/1 No. 4470 *Great Northern*, Works No. 1536, built in April 1922. She was the first of Gresley's Pacifics and was allocated to Doncaster shed. In May 1945 she entered the Plant where Thompson rebuilt her from Class A1 to A1/1, returning to traffic in September 1945. Later that year she was back at the Plant for a light repair when this photograph was taken on Thursday 13 December. She was withdrawn as BR No. 60113 in November 1962.

FIG. 40   DON 46/62

Thompson A2 No. 511 *Airborne*, Works No. 2002, built in July 1946 and allocated to Gateshead. Posing for her official photograph on Friday 19 July 1946, the day before she went into traffic. She was withdrawn as BR No. 60511 in November 1962.

FIG. 41   DON 46/63

A close up view of *Airborne's* motion. Note the sand box filler pipes with trays to catch any spillage.

FIG. 42   DON 47/180

A Peppercorn A2 (number not recorded) in course of erection in E2 shop at the Plant on Thursday 26 November 1947.

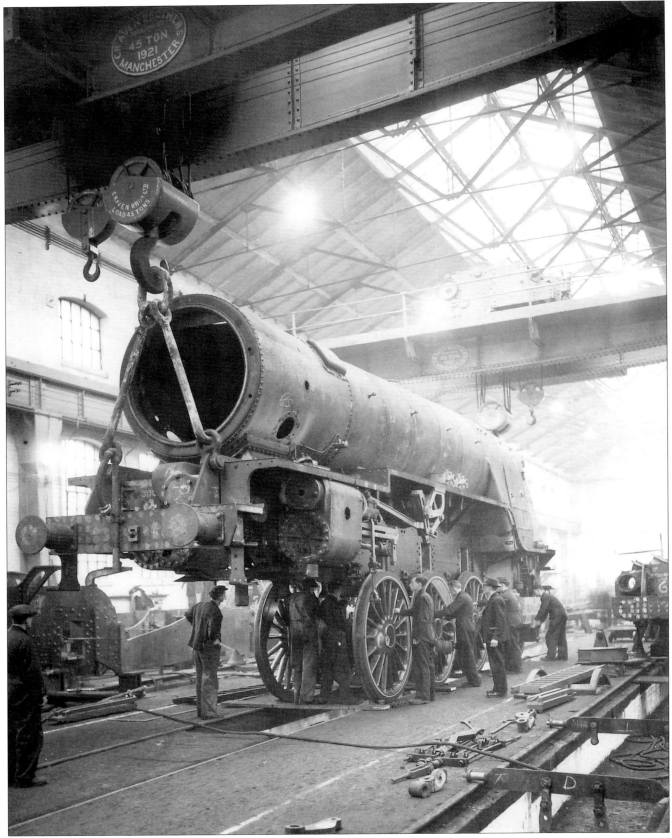

FIG. 43
DON 48/11

This photograph, taken on Thursday 15 January 1948, should really come under the British Railways era, but as she started life as an LNER engine it was thought appropriate to include it here. Peppercorn Class A2 (number not recorded) is shown receiving her driving wheels in E2 shop at the Plant. They are already painted apple green and lined out in black and white, the standard LNER livery. All 15 engines of Class A2 were painted in LNER livery, but only the first two carried the company initials, the remainder being lettered 'British Railways'. The travelling cranes were built by Craven Bros Ltd of Manchester in 1921 and were capable of lifting up to 90 tons between them.

FIG. 44

DON 47/185

Peppercorn A2 No. 525 *A. H. Peppercorn*, Works No. 2016, built in December 1947 and allocated to Doncaster shed. Photographed in 'H' shop at the Plant whilst being undercoated on Wednesday 26 November 1947.

FIG. 45

DON 47/205

A2 No. 525 just out of the paint shop on Monday 15 December 1947. All 15 engines of the class received LNER livery but only the first two, 525 *A. H. Peppercorn* and 526 *Sugar Palm*, carried LNER on their tenders. The remaining 13 were lettered British Railways. She was withdrawn as BR No. 60525 in March 1963.

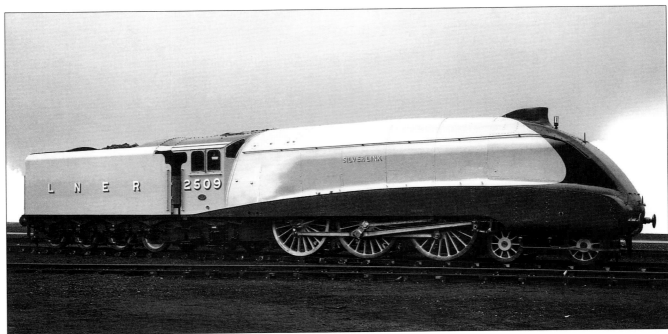

FIG. 46   DON 35/165

A4 No. 2509 *Silver Link*, Works No. 1818, built in September 1935 and allocated to King's Cross. The first of the Silver engine quartet built for operating 'The Silver Jubilee' train. She was shedded overnight at Gateshead when the service first commenced. The following November she was back at the Plant for a light repair when this photograph was taken. She worked the service on her own for the first three weeks until No. 2510 *Quicksilver* was completed and able to take her turn. She was withdrawn as BR No. 60014 in December 1962.

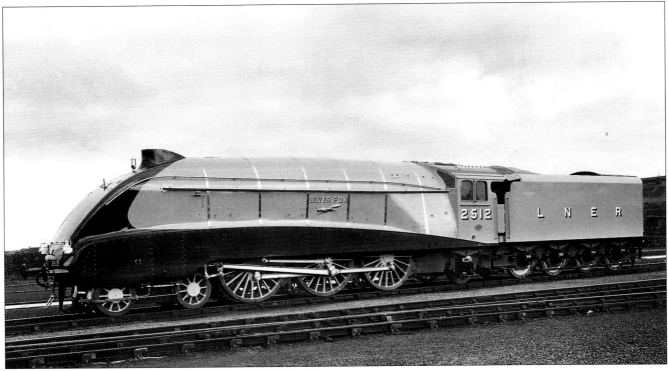

FIG. 47   DON 36/183

A4 No. 2512 *Silver Fox*, Works No. 1823, built in December 1935 and allocated to King's Cross. She was the last of the four Silver engines for working the 'Silver Jubilee' train and differed from her sisters in having stainless steel boiler bands and a stainless steel fox beneath her name. After *Silver Link*, all the A4s had boiler hand rails which curved down towards the cab following the profile of the side valances. She is shown here at the Plant on Monday 28 September 1936 having just undergone a heavy repair. She was withdrawn as BR No. 60017 in October 1963.

FIG. 48

AUTHOR'S COLLECTION

Whilst not shown in colour (the original is in royal blue and silver) this company publicity booklet, like the two reproduced later, is worthy of inclusion for the amount of information it contains. The inaugural service was on Friday 27 September 1935.

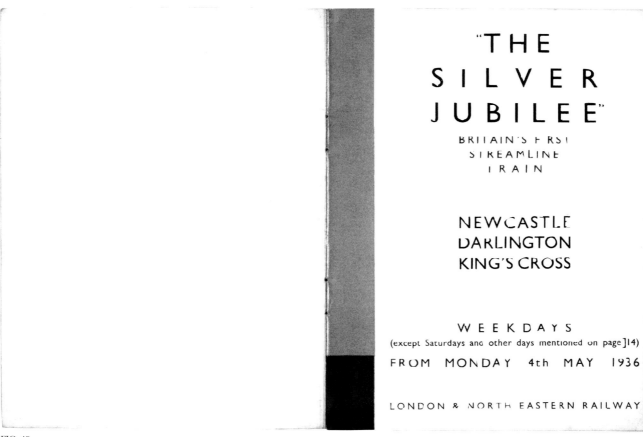

FIG. 49

AUTHOR'S COLLECTION

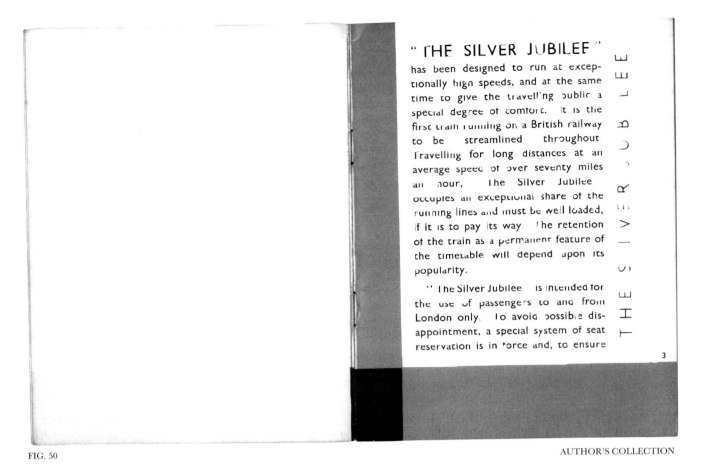

"THE SILVER JUBILEE" has been designed to run at exceptionally high speeds, and at the same time to give the travelling public a special degree of comfort. It is the first train running on a British railway to be streamlined throughout. Travelling for long distances at an average speed of over seventy miles an hour, The Silver Jubilee occupies an exceptional share of the running lines and must be well loaded, if it is to pay its way. The retention of the train as a permanent feature of the timetable will depend upon its popularity.

"The Silver Jubilee" is intended for the use of passengers to and from London only. To avoid possible disappointment, a special system of seat reservation is in force and, to ensure

3

FIG. 50

AUTHOR'S COLLECTION

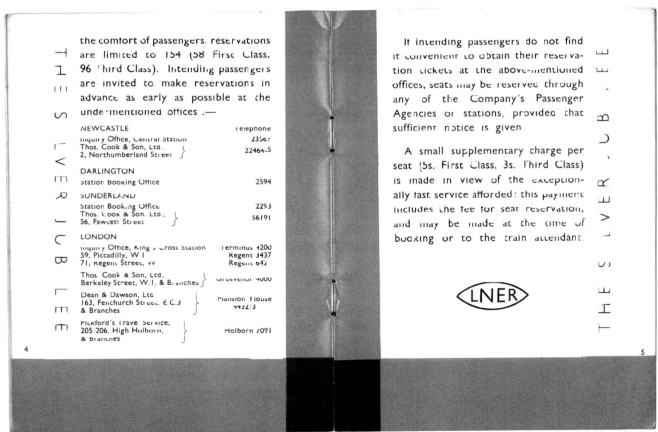

the comfort of passengers, reservations are limited to 154 (58 First Class, 96 Third Class). Intending passengers are invited to make reservations in advance as early as possible at the undermentioned offices.—

NEWCASTLE	Telephone
Inquiry Office, Central Station	23567
Thos. Cook & Son, Ltd., 2, Northumberland Street	22464-5
DARLINGTON	
Station Booking Office	2594
SUNDERLAND	
Station Booking Office	2293
Thos. Cook & Son. Ltd., 56, Fawcett Street	56191
LONDON	
Inquiry Office, King's Cross Station	Terminus 4200
59, Piccadilly, W.1	Regent 3437
71, Regent Street, W	Regent 642
Thos. Cook & Son, Ltd., Berkeley Street, W.1, & Branches	Grosvenor 4000
Dean & Dawson, Ltd, 163, Fenchurch Street, E.C.3 & Branches	Mansion House 4432/3
Pickford's Travel Service, 205/206, High Holborn, & Branches	Holborn 7091

It intending passengers do not find it convenient to obtain their reservation tickets at the above-mentioned offices, seats may be reserved through any of the Company's Passenger Agencies or stations, provided that sufficient notice is given.

A small supplementary charge per seat (5s. First Class, 3s. Third Class) is made in view of the exceptionally fast service afforded: this payment includes the fee for seat reservation, and may be made at the time of booking or to the train attendant.

LNER

4

5

FIG. 51

AUTHOR'S COLLECTION

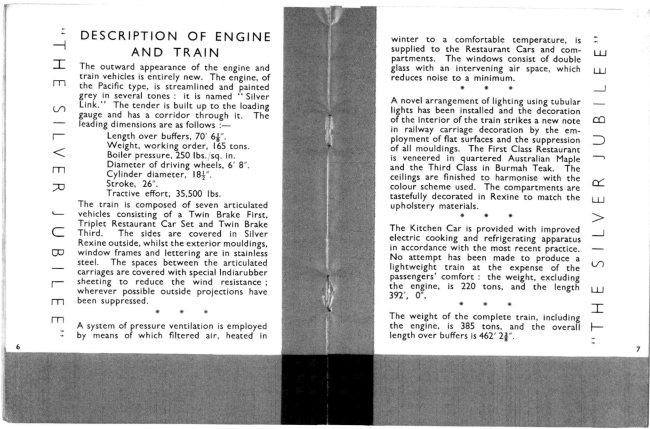

DESCRIPTION OF ENGINE AND TRAIN

The outward appearance of the engine and train vehicles is entirely new. The engine, of the Pacific type, is streamlined and painted grey in several tones : it is named " Silver Link." The tender is built up to the loading gauge and has a corridor through it. The leading dimensions are as follows :—

Length over buffers, 70′ 6⅛″.
Weight, working order, 165 tons.
Boiler pressure, 250 lbs./sq. in.
Diameter of driving wheels, 6′ 8″.
Cylinder diameter, 18½″.
Stroke, 26″.
Tractive effort, 35,500 lbs.

The train is composed of seven articulated vehicles consisting of a Twin Brake First, Triplet Restaurant Car Set and Twin Brake Third. The sides are covered in Silver Rexine outside, whilst the exterior mouldings, window frames and lettering are in stainless steel. The spaces between the articulated carriages are covered with special Indiarubber sheeting to reduce the wind resistance ; wherever possible outside projections have been suppressed.

* * *

A system of pressure ventilation is employed by means of which filtered air, heated in winter to a comfortable temperature, is supplied to the Restaurant Cars and compartments. The windows consist of double glass with an intervening air space, which reduces noise to a minimum.

* * *

A novel arrangement of lighting using tubular lights has been installed and the decoration of the interior of the train strikes a new note in railway carriage decoration by the employment of flat surfaces and the suppression of all mouldings. The First Class Restaurant is veneered in quartered Australian Maple and the Third Class in Burmah Teak. The ceilings are finished to harmonise with the colour scheme used. The compartments are tastefully decorated in Rexine to match the upholstery materials.

* * *

The Kitchen Car is provided with improved electric cooking and refrigerating apparatus in accordance with the most recent practice. No attempt has been made to produce a lightweight train at the expense of the passengers' comfort : the weight, excluding the engine, is 220 tons, and the length 392′, 0″.

* * *

The weight of the complete train, including the engine, is 385 tons, and the overall length over buffers is 462′ 2⅜″.

FIG. 52

AUTHOR'S COLLECTION

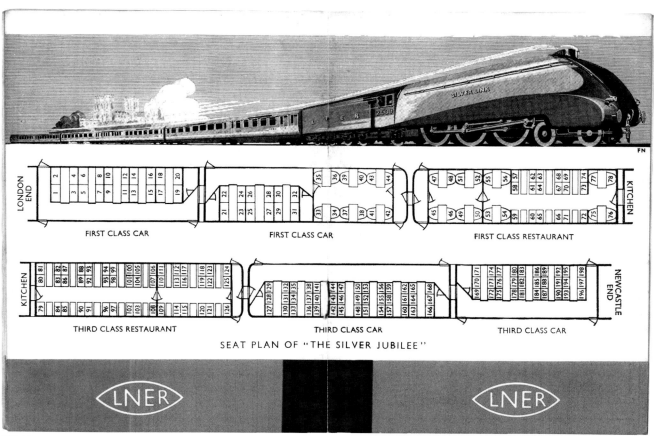

SEAT PLAN OF "THE SILVER JUBILEE"

FIG. 53

AUTHOR'S COLLECTION

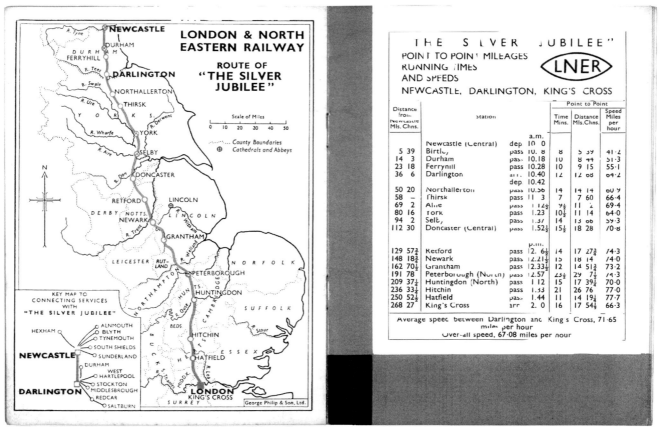

FIG. 54   AUTHOR'S COLLECTION

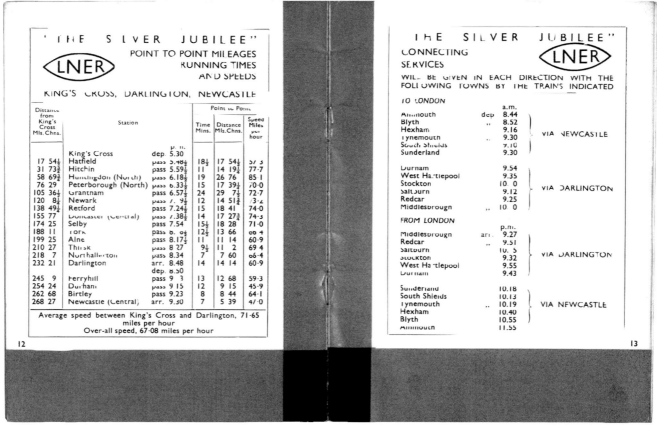

FIG. 55   AUTHOR'S COLLECTION

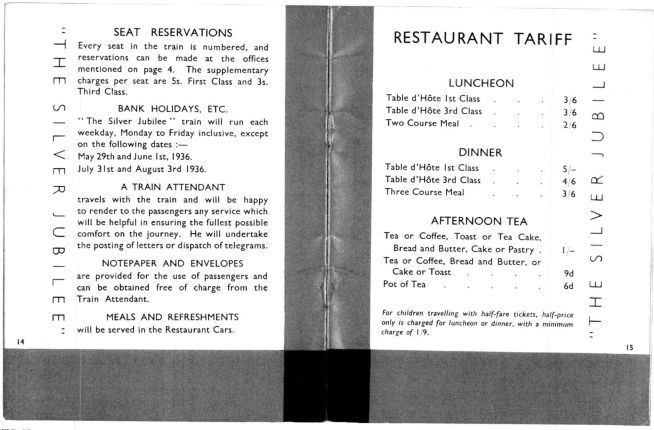

THE SILVER JUBILEE

SEAT RESERVATIONS

Every seat in the train is numbered, and reservations can be made at the offices mentioned on page 4. The supplementary charges per seat are 5s. First Class and 3s. Third Class.

BANK HOLIDAYS, ETC.

"The Silver Jubilee" train will run each weekday, Monday to Friday inclusive, except on the following dates :—

May 29th and June 1st, 1936.
July 31st and August 3rd 1936.

A TRAIN ATTENDANT

travels with the train and will be happy to render to the passengers any service which will be helpful in ensuring the fullest possible comfort on the journey. He will undertake the posting of letters or dispatch of telegrams.

NOTEPAPER AND ENVELOPES

are provided for the use of passengers and can be obtained free of charge from the Train Attendant.

MEALS AND REFRESHMENTS

will be served in the Restaurant Cars.

14

RESTAURANT TARIFF

"THE SILVER JUBILEE"

LUNCHEON

Table d'Hôte 1st Class	3/6
Table d'Hôte 3rd Class	3/6
Two Course Meal	2/6

DINNER

Table d'Hôte 1st Class	5/–
Table d'Hôte 3rd Class	4/6
Three Course Meal	3/6

AFTERNOON TEA

Tea or Coffee, Toast or Tea Cake, Bread and Butter, Cake or Pastry	1/–
Tea or Coffee, Bread and Butter, or Cake or Toast	9d
Pot of Tea	6d

For children travelling with half-fare tickets, half-price only is charged for luncheon or dinner, with a minimum charge of 1/9.

15

FIG. 56

AUTHOR'S COLLECTION

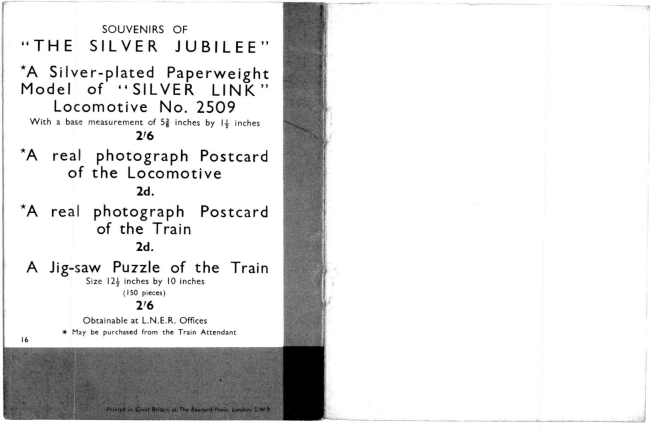

SOUVENIRS OF

"THE SILVER JUBILEE"

A Silver-plated Paperweight Model of "SILVER LINK" Locomotive No. 2509

With a base measurement of 5¾ inches by 1½ inches

2/6

*A real photograph Postcard of the Locomotive

2d.

*A real photograph Postcard of the Train

2d.

A Jig-saw Puzzle of the Train

Size 12½ inches by 10 inches
(150 pieces)

2/6

Obtainable at L.N.E.R. Offices
* May be purchased from the Train Attendant

16

Printed in Great Britain at The Baynard Press, London, S.W.9

FIG. 57

AUTHOR'S COLLECTION

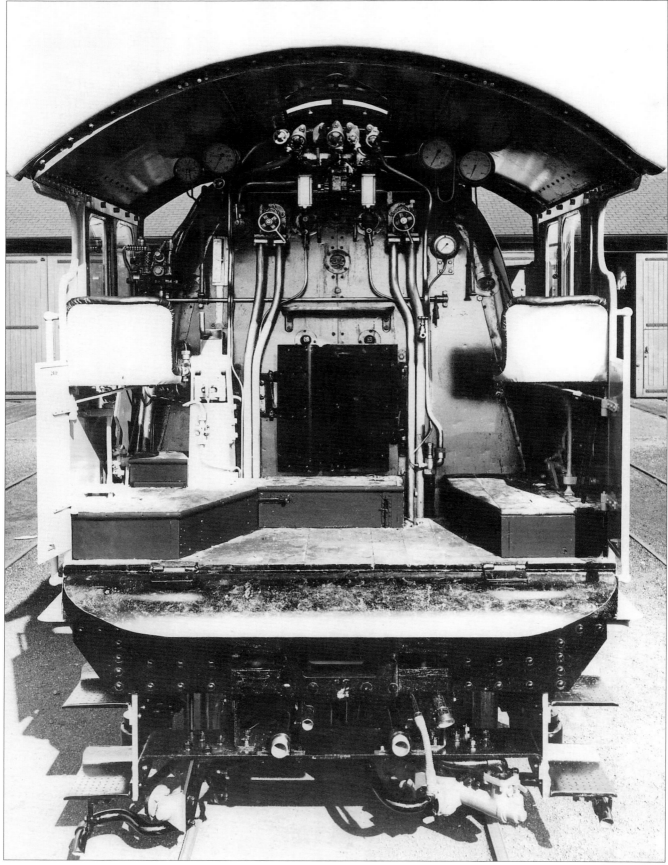

FIG. 58   DON 35/136

Inside the cab of No. 2509 *Silver Link* taken at the plant in September 1935. There is a face plate injector just below and to the side of each of the twin water gauges. The horizontal shaft above the fire hole door actuates the whistle, easily to hand for both driver and fireman. Later A4s had slightly higher round-topped backs to the seats. When originally fitted, the speed recorder sat on the step beneath the fireman's seat on the right in a convenient position for the driver.

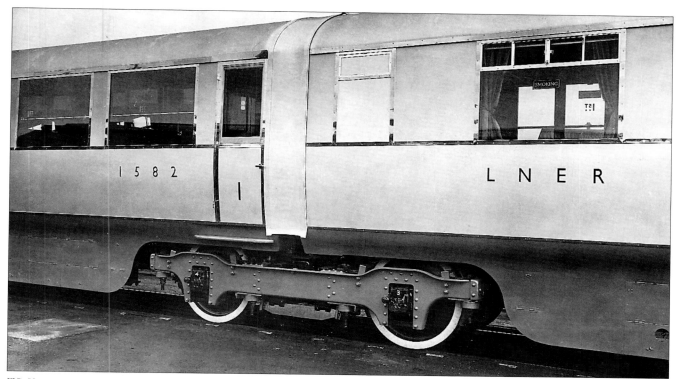

FIG. 59

DON 35/146

'The Silver Jubilee' First-class semi-open brake end articulated coaches Nos. 1582 and 1581. The photograph, taken at the Plant in October 1935, was intended to show the India rubber covering between the coaches. 'The Silver Jubilee' train of seven vehicles and the four locomotives cost the company £34,500. The return for the first year, received from the five shilling and three shilling supplements which were charged on top of the normal ticket price, was £12,000. In the first year 498 journeys were made between Newcastle and London. The one set of vehicles made every journey except for one day and covered 133,000 miles. Passenger loadings averaged 137 persons per trip, which gave 86 per cent occupation of seats throughout the year.

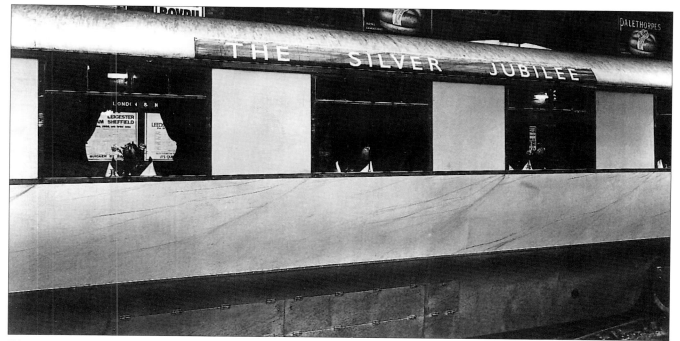

FIG. 60

AUTHOR'S COLLECTION

A close-up view of one of 'The Silver Jubilee' coaches after arrival at King's Cross. Great care was taken with the appearance of the train which was washed down and leathered prior to each journey. It is interesting to see just how dirty it became after one trip from Newcastle, with the dirt thrown up from the bogies, and the sooty roof. The coach sides were covered with a light silver-grey rexine with a darker grey paint on the underframes and bogies. All strips, letters and numerals were in stainless steel and the roof was spray-painted in silver. The overall effect was a train of striking appearance.

FIG. 61 (LEFT)   AUTHOR'S COLLECTION

A4 No. 2512 *Silver Fox* at King's Cross on a winter's evening in 1937. With her blower hard on, she awaits her 5.30 p.m. departure for Newcastle where she is due in at 9.30 p.m.

FIG. 62 (BELOW)   L. HANSON

A4 No. 2509 *Silver Link* approaching Sandy on Saturday 1 May 1937 at the head of the up junior 'Flying Scotsman'. This was a balancing turn to get her back to King's Cross. K3 No. 229, also a King's Cross engine at this time, sits waiting for a path through the Sandy station bottleneck. It was not unusual for goods trains to have to wait up to 20 minutes, occasionally very much longer, depending on the time of day. No. 229 was built at Darlington in 1925 and was withdrawn as BR No. 61868 in May 1952.

FIG. 63   DON 37/36

Scale model of A4 No. 2509 Silver Link which the company had built, possibly by Bassett-Lowke Ltd of Northampton, for display on their stand at the 1937 Paris Exhibition. No scale is given, but ¾ inch to 1 foot would seem to be a likely choice. Photographed in April 1937.

FIG. 64   DON 35/145   FIG. 65   DON 28/64

A4 No. 2510 *Quicksilver*, Works No. 1819, built in September 1935 and allocated to King's Cross. This front view, taken when she was new at the Plant, shows well the recessed draw hook which, with short buffers, presented a hazard when coupling up. This problem only applied to the four Silver engines and they were later modified. *Quicksilver* was withdrawn as BR No. 60015 in April 1963.

A corridor tender of the type that would have been fitted to A1 No. 4476 *Royal Lancer*. (See accident report overleaf.) Note the metal plate across the bottom of the corridor gangway which was instrumental in causing the death of Fireman Lawton. Photographed at the Plant on Tuesday 15 May 1928.

FATAL ACCIDENT AT KINGS CROSS ON 10 FEBRUARY 1936

Mention has been made on a number of occasions of the accident which occurred at King's Cross station in 1936 because of the short buffers and recessed draw hook giving insufficient room for a man to carry out the coupling or uncoupling of the engine. There has been mention of this event from time to time in books or articles, mostly incorrect and certainly with wrong dates quoted. The copy of the official accident report below is of interest, more so as it was to change the frontal appearance of all A4s built after the four Silver engines.

MINISTRY OF TRANSPORT RAILWAY ACCIDENT REPORT
Reproduced by kind permission of H. M. Railway Inspectorate

SIR,

I have the honour to report for the information of the Minister of Transport, in accordance with the Order of the 6th March, 1936, the result of my Inquiry into the circumstances attending the fatal accident which occurred on the 10th February, 1936, to V. Lawton at King's Cross on the London and North Eastern Railway.

Lawton, who was employed as a fireman, was acting as such to Driver Peachey on Engine No. 4476 which was booked to run light from King's Cross Locomotive Depot to the Passenger Station, and work the 5.45 p.m. express passenger train thence to Newcastle. In order to reduce track occupation this engine left the depot coupled to streamlined Engine No. 2512 which was due to leave King's Cross 15 minutes earlier. As both were travelling tender first and the streamlined engine was leading, the smoke box end of that engine was coupled to the tender of the other, which was fitted with a corridor. On arrival at the station they were brought to a stand alongside No. 6 platform, and it was Lawton's duty to release the coupling.

He alighted on to the ballast from his own side of the footplate, and after parting the vacuum pipes placed that of Engine No. 4476 on the plug. He then called from between the engines to Joseph Holland, the fireman of the streamlined engine, who was arranging the smoke box head lamps thereof, and requested him to ask Peachey to ease up. Holland took a few paces towards the footplate of Engine No. 4476 to pass on the message and by the time he got back to Lawton the easing up movement had taken place and he found him with his head crushed between the lower edge of the corridor gangway, which is of the Pullman type, and the streamline plating. Death had been instantaneous.

When in their normal positions the faces of these gangways and of the buffers are in the same vertical plane. They are kept there by springs with the result that when the buffers are compressed against those of a non-corridor vehicle, as in this instance, the gangway remains fully extended. As the plating at the front of a streamlined engine is only seven inches behind the buffer faces, this figure represents the clearance between it and the face of the vestibule when the buffers are just touching, and a normal easing up movement reduces this space to three inches or even less.

Lawton, who worked both types of engines frequently, was doubtless aware of this danger, and I am of opinion that in the effort of lifting the shackle off the draw bar hook, which he succeeded in doing, he inadvertently raised his head at the same time, with the results already described.

His action in remaining between the engines was contrary to Rule 12 (b) which directs that "Employees must not remain between vehicles or engines when a gangway or gangways interpose during an 'easing up' movement, but must stand clear of such vehicles or engines until they are at rest." He was in possession of a Rule Book, and as he disregarded this rule he must be held responsible for the accident.

It is also to be regretted that Holland, who admits that he was aware of this rule, did not wait to see that Lawton complied with it before he asked Peachey to ease up.

As a result of this accident, the buffers and drawgear at the front of the streamlined engines are being lengthened by nine inches to provide more space for the men engaged in coupling and uncoupling.

It should be noted, however, that this alteration in design will in no way affect the necessity for complying strictly with the Rule, which I have quoted, on every occasion when a gangway interposes.

In view of the importance of this rule, and the fact that until the advent of corridor tenders it did not concern the majority of enginemen, I recommend that the attention of the men be specially drawn to it by notices at Locomotive Depots.

I have, etc.,

J. L. M. MOORE.

MORE STREAMLINED TRAINS

The success of their first streamlined train 'The Silver Jubilee', both in passenger loadings and the publicity it generated for the company, gave birth to the idea of introducing two further trains – 'The Coronation' in 1937 and the 'West Riding Limited' in 1938. 'The Coronation' differed from the other two in as much as two trains were run each day in the up and down direction connecting London and Edinburgh. 'The Silver Jubilee' offered a day return service between

Newcastle and London and the 'West Riding Limited' between Bradford and London. The publicity brochures for both these trains are reproduced in the following pages for the details that they contain. They are most strikingly coloured, that of 'The Coronation' being in red and gold whilst the 'West Riding Limited' has blue as the prominent colour.

FIG. 66

DON 37/92

A4 No. 4488 *Union of South Africa*, Works No. 1853, built in June 1937 and allocated to Haymarket. She was the first of the five engines to be built for working the new 'Coronation' streamlined trains, and the first engine to appear in the garter blue livery. Here she is seen after making her debut from the paint shop on Tuesday 22 June 1937. She was withdrawn as BR No. 60009 in June 1966.

AUTHOR'S COLLECTION
A luggage label from The Coronation train
reproduced actual size.

FIG. 67   AUTHOR'S COLLECTION

The inaugural service was on Monday 5 July 1937.

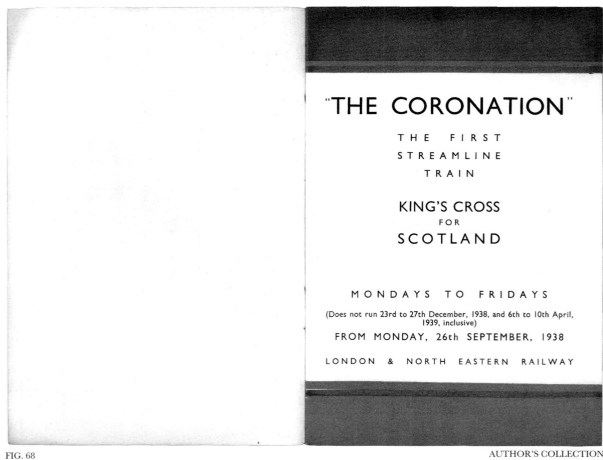

FIG. 68   AUTHOR'S COLLECTION

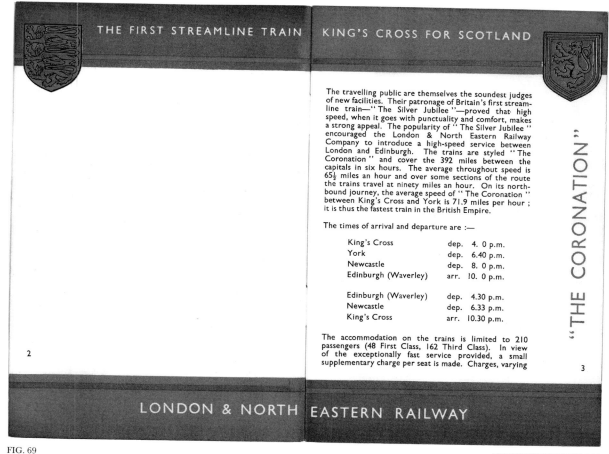

FIG. 69

AUTHOR'S COLLECTION

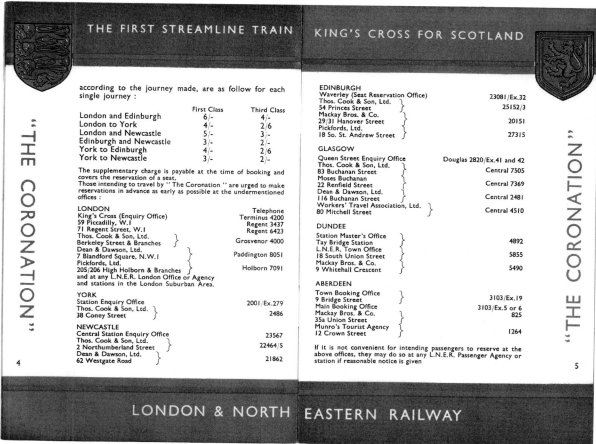

FIG. 70

AUTHOR'S COLLECTION

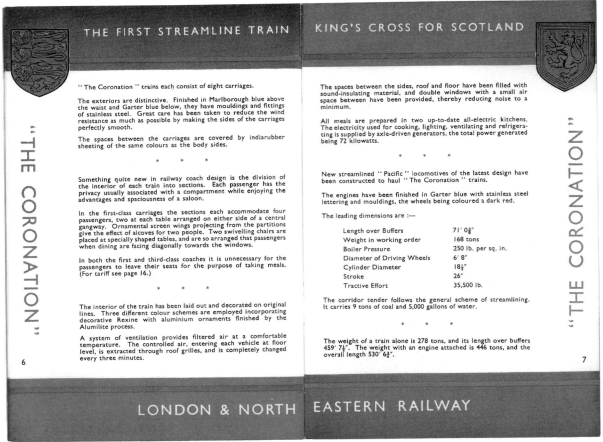

"THE CORONATION"

"The Coronation" trains each consist of eight carriages.

The exteriors are distinctive. Finished in Marlborough blue above the waist and Garter blue below, they have mouldings and fittings of stainless steel. Great care has been taken to reduce the wind resistance as much as possible by making the sides of the carriages perfectly smooth.

The spaces between the carriages are covered by indiarubber sheeting of the same colours as the body sides.

* * *

Something quite new in railway coach design is the division of the interior of each train into sections. Each passenger has the privacy usually associated with a compartment while enjoying the advantages and spaciousness of a saloon.

In the first-class carriages the sections each accommodate four passengers, two at each table arranged on either side of a central gangway. Ornamental screen wings projecting from the partitions give the effect of alcoves for two people. Two swivelling chairs are placed at specially shaped tables, and are so arranged that passengers when dining are facing diagonally towards the windows.

In both the first and third-class coaches it is unnecessary for the passengers to leave their seats for the purpose of taking meals. (For tariff see page 16.)

* * *

The interior of the train has been laid out and decorated on original lines. Three different colour schemes are employed incorporating decorative Rexine with aluminium ornaments finished by the Alumilite process.

A system of ventilation provides filtered air at a comfortable temperature. The controlled air, entering each vehicle at floor level, is extracted through roof grilles, and is completely changed every three minutes.

6

The spaces between the sides, roof and floor have been filled with sound-insulating material, and double windows with a small air space between have been provided, thereby reducing noise to a minimum.

All meals are prepared in two up-to-date all-electric kitchens. The electricity used for cooking, lighting, ventilating and refrigerating is supplied by axle-driven generators, the total power generated being 72 kilowatts.

* * *

New streamlined "Pacific" locomotives of the latest design have been constructed to haul "The Coronation" trains.

The engines have been finished in Garter blue with stainless steel lettering and mouldings, the wheels being coloured a dark red.

The leading dimensions are :—

Length over Buffers	71' 0⅜"
Weight in working order	168 tons
Boiler Pressure	250 lb. per sq. in.
Diameter of Driving Wheels	6' 8"
Cylinder Diameter	18½"
Stroke	26"
Tractive Effort	35,500 lb.

The corridor tender follows the general scheme of streamlining. It carries 9 tons of coal and 5,000 gallons of water.

* * *

The weight of a train alone is 278 tons, and its length over buffers 459' 7½". The weight with an engine attached is 446 tons, and the overall length 530' 6¾".

7

LONDON & NORTH EASTERN RAILWAY

FIG. 71

AUTHOR'S COLLECTION

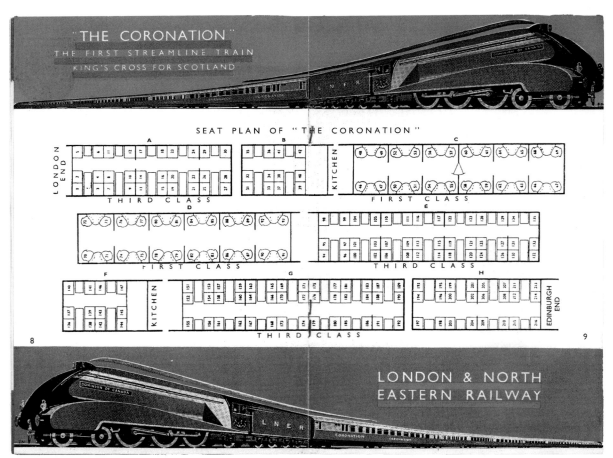

"THE CORONATION"
THE FIRST STREAMLINE TRAIN
KING'S CROSS FOR SCOTLAND

SEAT PLAN OF "THE CORONATION"

LONDON & NORTH EASTERN RAILWAY

FIG. 72

AUTHOR'S COLLECTION

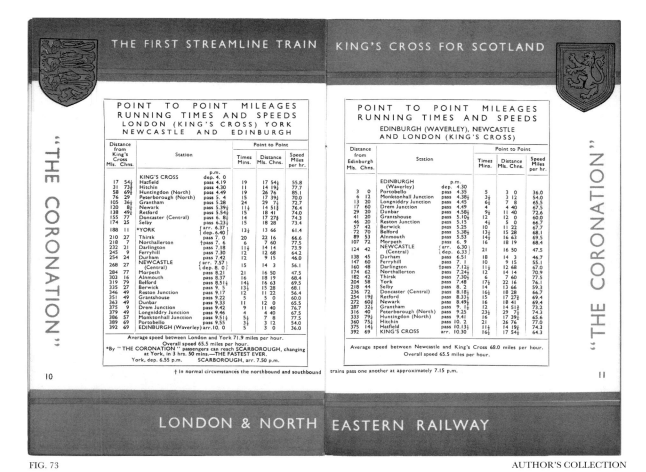

FIG. 73 AUTHOR'S COLLECTION

FIG. 74 AUTHOR'S COLLECTION

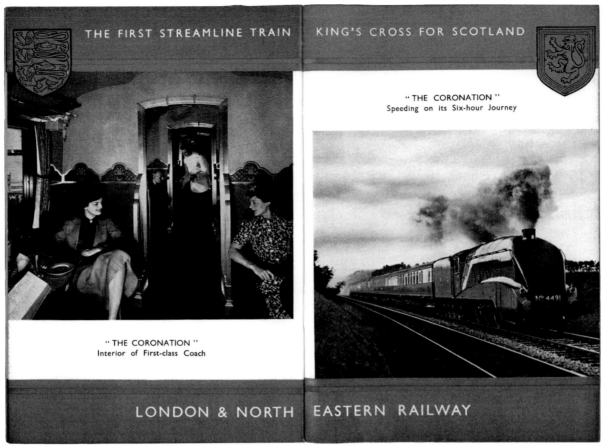

FIG. 75   AUTHOR'S COLLECTION

RESTAURANT TARIFF

AFTERNOON TEA

Tea or Coffee, Toast or Tea Cake. Bread and Butter. Cake or Pastry	1/-
Tea or Coffee, Bread and Butter, or Cake or Toast	9d
Pot of Tea	6d

DINNER

Table d'Hôte First Class	5/-
Table d'Hôte Third Class	4/6

À LA CARTE MEALS ALSO AVAILABLE

For children travelling with half-fare tickets, half-price only is charged for dinner or à la carte meals, with a minimum charge of 1/9.

TRAIN ATTENDANTS

travel with the train and will be happy to render to the passengers any service which will be helpful in ensuring the fullest possible comfort on the journey. They will undertake the posting of letters or dispatch of telegrams.

POSTCARD PHOTOGRAPHS

of the train and streamlined locomotives can be obtained (price twopence each) from the Attendant.

16

Printed in Great Britain   *The Baynard Press*

FIG. 76   AUTHOR'S COLLECTION

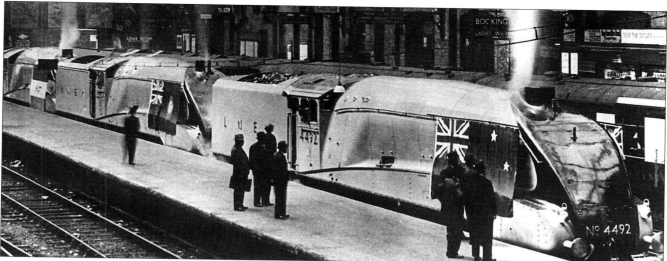

FIG. 77

AUTHOR'S COLLECTION

A4s (left to right) No. 4488 *Union of South Africa*, No. 4490 *Empire of India* and No. 4492 *Dominion of New Zealand*, await the arrival of the High Commissioners of the countries, after which the engines were named to take part in a combined naming ceremony at King's Cross on Monday 28 June 1937.

FIG. 78

L. HANSON

A4 No. 4488 *Union of South Africa* passing through Princes Street Gardens on her way into Edinburgh's Waverley station on Wednesday 4 August 1938.

DON 37/112

FIG. 79

The first observation coach to be completed, No. 1719, in a specially posed photograph of 'The Coronation' train on the up slow line at Retford in July 1937. Whilst the coach certainly added to the appearance of the train it was really only of publicity value since when journeys began the train was carrying a coach with 16 empty seats which were then available at a shilling per hour session (five sessions per journey) to passengers who already had seats on the train. A total maximum income of £4 per trip – not exactly commercially viable.

DON 37/51

FIG. 80

Observation saloons Nos. 1719 and 1729 under construction in the carriage shop on Thursday 20 May 1937. Both were built to Diagram 232, weighed 34 tons apiece and cost £4,367 each. The transparent curved rear windows were specially moulded in Perspex by ICI who at that time were involved in making many different shapes and sizes of cockpit covers for the aircraft industry. 'The Coronation' was the only streamlined train to include observation cars in their formations and these were only run in the summer months.

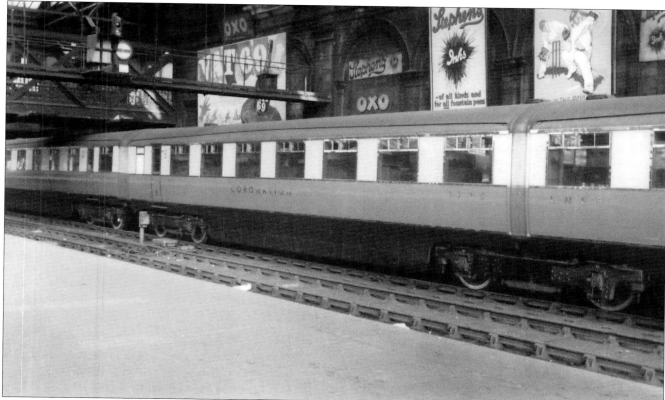

FIG. 81

L. HANSON

Articulated 'Coronation' coach No. 1725, built in 1937, standing in Edinburgh (Waverley) on Thursday 4 August 1938. The name 'CORONATION' on each coach was in 6 in. Gill Sans lettering, whilst the running numbers were in 4 in. numerals. They were all, together with the trim lines, in stainless steel. The contrast between the Marlborough blue above the waistline and the Garter blue finish beneath it shows up well in this photograph. Three Coronation train sets were built, one each for the up and down services and a third, finished in the same colours but without the name 'Coronation', as a spare should it be required for any of the three streamlined services.

FIG. 82

DON 37/71

A4 No. 4489 *Dominion of Canada*, Works No. 1854, built in May 1937 and allocated to King's Cross. For two weeks she carried the name *Woodcock* before returning to the Plant to receive her new nameplates and added embellishments to make her the second of the special engines for working 'The Coronation' trains. Photographed on Friday 11 June 1937. Her naming ceremony took place at King's Cross on Tuesday 15 June 1937 by the Canadian High Commissioner. She was withdrawn as BR No. 60010 in May 1965. After cosmetic restoration she was presented to the Acting High Commissioner for Canada who accepted her on behalf of the Canadian Railroad Historical Society for exhibition in their museum at Delson near Montreal.

FIG. 83

L. HANSON

A4 No. 4490 *Empire of India*, Works No. 1855, built in June 1937 and allocated to King's Cross. Some five months later she was reallocated to Haymarket where she is seen on the turntable on Thursday 4 August 1938. She was withdrawn as BR No. 60011 in May 1964.

FIG. 84

L. HANSON

A4 No. 4492 *Dominion of New Zealand*, a King's Cross engine with driver Nash, seen departing from platform 5 at King's Cross on the down 'Coronation' at 4 p.m. on Tuesday 19 April 1938. She was due into York, her only stop, at 6.37 p.m. before continuing her journey to Edinburgh where she was due at 10 p.m.

FIG. 85

DON 37/110

A4 No. 4492 *Dominion of New Zealand*, Works No. 1857, built in June 1937 and allocated to King's Cross. This posed photograph shows her stationary on the up slow line at Retford with 'The Coronation' train in July 1937. She was withdrawn as BR No. 60013 in April 1963.

Each of the five engines allocated to work the 'Coronation' service was named after a member country of the British Empire. With the consent of the countries concerned, each carried the respective armorial bearing hand-painted on a steel plate and fixed to the cab side beneath the stainless steel numerals. Here, three of these are illustrated. As they occupied the position of the makers' plates, these were repositioned inside the cab.

FIG. 86   DON 37/58

The coat of arms of the Dominion of Canada as displayed on the cab sides of A4 engine No. 4489 *Dominion of Canada.*

FIG. 87   DON 37/73

The coat of arms of the Empire of India as displayed on the cab sides of A4 engine No. 4490 *Empire of India.*

FIG. 88   DON 37/61

The coat of arms of the Dominion of New Zealand as displayed on the cab sides of A4 engine No. 4492 *Dominion of New Zealand.*

FIG. 89   DON 37/146

A4 No. 4495 *Golden Fleece*, Works No. 1860, built in August 1937 and allocated to King's Cross. When she first emerged from the Plant she was in green livery and named *Great Snipe*. After a few weeks she was chosen to be one of the two engines to haul the 'West Riding Limited', so she was returned to the Plant and repainted in the Garter Blue livery with stainless steel and chromed embellishments, and given the name *Golden Fleece* which was more appropriate to the wool trade. Photographed just out of the paint shop on Monday 27 September 1937. She was withdrawn as BR No. 60030 in December 1962.

FIG. 90   DON 37/143

A4 No. 4496 *Golden Shuttle*, Works No. 1861, built in September 1937 and allocated to King's Cross. She was the second of the pair of engines required to work the 'West Riding Limited' and was finished in Garter Blue with the stainless steel and chromed embellishments from new. Photographed on Monday 27 September 1937. She was withdrawn as BR No. 60008 in July 1963.

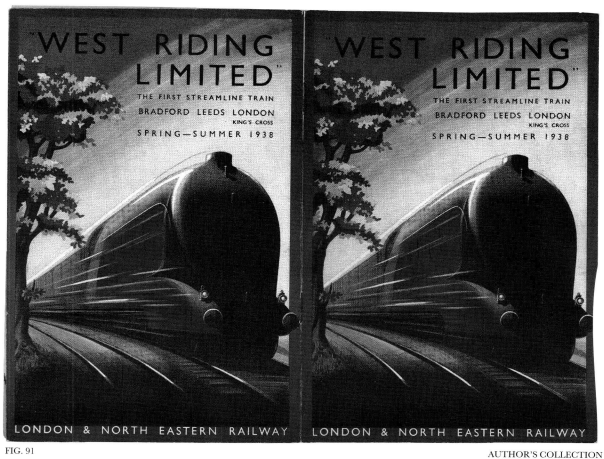

FIG. 91

AUTHOR'S COLLECTION

Rear and front cover. The inaugural service was on Monday 27 September 1937.

FIG. 92

AUTHOR'S COLLECTION

"WEST RIDING LIMITED"

Since their inception the L.N.E.R. streamline train services between London and Newcastle (" The Silver Jubilee ") and London and Edinburgh (" The Coronation ") have won their place in the list of the world's most famous trains. With every confidence in the public patronage of further services of this character, combining high speed with high standard of comfort and punctuality, the London & North Eastern Railway Company introduced the " West Riding Limited " between London, Leeds and Bradford.

The times of departure and arrival are :—

Bradford (Exchange)	dep.	11.10 a.m.
Leeds (Central)	dep.	11.31 a.m.
London (King's Cross)	arr.	2.15 p.m.
London (King's Cross)	dep.	7.10 p.m.
Leeds (Central)	arr.	9.53 p.m.
Bradford (Exchange)	arr.	10.15 p.m.

(See pages 10 and 11 for Mileage Tables.)

The "West Riding Limited " is intended for the use of passengers to and from London only.

3

THE FIRST STREAMLINE TRAIN
BRADFORD LEEDS AND LONDON (KING'S CROSS)

FIG. 93

AUTHOR'S COLLECTION

"WEST RIDING LIMITED" THE FIRST STREAMLINE TRAIN BETWEEN

The accommodation on the trains is limited to 210 passengers (48 First Class, 162 Third Class). In view of the exceptionally fast service provided, a small supplementary charge per seat is made. Charges are as follows for each single journey.

	First Class	Third Class
Bradford and London	4/-	2/6
Leeds and London	4/-	2/6

The supplementary charge, payable at the time of booking, covers the reservation of a seat.

Those intending to travel by the " West Riding Limited " are urged to make reservations in advance as early as possible at the following offices :

LONDON	Telephone
King's Cross (Enquiry Office)	Terminus 4200 Ex. 3610
59 Piccadilly, W.1	Regent 3437
71 Regent Street, W.1	Regent 6423
Thos. Cook & Son, Ltd. Berkeley Street & Branches	Grosvenor 4000
Dean & Dawson, Ltd., 7 Blandford Square, N.W.1, and Branches	Paddington 8051
Pickfords, Ltd., 205/206 High Holborn & Branches	Holborn 7091
and at any L.N.E.R. London Office or Agency and stations in the London Suburban Area.	

4

LEEDS	Telephone
Central Station (Booking Office)	30091
Thos. Cook & Son, Ltd., 55 Boar Lane	29071
Dean & Dawson, Ltd. 137 Briggate	30321/2
Messrs. A. Altham, 4 Newmarket Street	22147
Mr. A. W. Ivey, 11 Trinity Street	27860

BRADFORD	Telephone
Exchange Station (Booking Office)	9446 or 1369
Thos. Cook & Son, Ltd., 19 Market Street	8144
Dean & Dawson, Ltd. 24 Market Street	1114/5
Messrs. Briggs & Hill, 70 Market Street	4030
Messrs. A. Altham, 21 Westgate	8526

HALIFAX	Telephone
Old Station (Booking Office)	4207
Messrs. A. Altham, 23 Woolshops	3402

HARROGATE	
Harrogate Station (Stationmaster's Office)	4378
Messrs. Dean & Dawson, 16 James Street	4155

HUDDERSFIELD	
Messrs. Dean & Dawson, 7 St. Peter's Street	571

If it is not convenient for intending passengers to reserve at the above offices, they may do so at any L.N.E.R. Passenger Agency or station if reasonable notice is given.

5

BRADFORD LEEDS AND LONDON

FIG. 94

AUTHOR'S COLLECTION

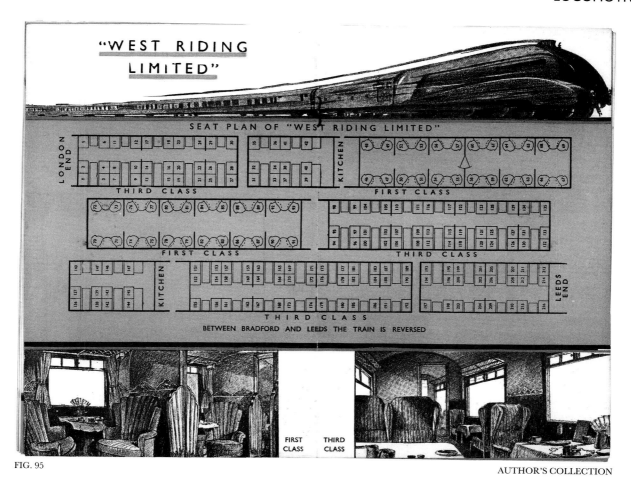

FIG. 95

AUTHOR'S COLLECTION

"WEST RIDING LIMITED" THE FIRST STREAMLINE TRAIN BETWEEN

The train consists of eight carriages. The exterior is distinctive.

Finished in Marlborough blue above the waist and Garter blue below, it has mouldings and fittings of stainless steel. Great care has been taken to reduce the wind resistance as much as possible by making the sides of the carriages perfectly smooth. The spaces between the carriages are covered by indiarubber sheeting of the same colours as the body sides.

* * *

Something quite new in railway coach design is the division of the interior of each train into sections. Each passenger has the privacy usually associated with a compartment while enjoying the advantages and spaciousness of a saloon.

In the first-class carriages the sections each accommodate four passengers, two at each table arranged on either side of a central gangway. Ornamental screen wings projecting from the partitions give the effect of alcoves for two people. Two swivelling chairs are placed at specially shaped tables, and are so arranged that passengers when dining are facing diagonally towards the windows.

In both the first and third-class coaches it is unnecessary for the passengers to leave their seats for the purpose of taking meals. (For tariff see page 12.)

* * *

The interior of the train has been laid out and decorated on original lines. Three different colour schemes are employed incorporating decorative Rexine with aluminium ornaments finished by the Alumilite process.

8

A system of ventilation provides filtered air at a comfortable temperature. The controlled air, entering each vehicle at floor level, is extracted through roof grilles, and is completely changed every three minutes.

The spaces between the sides, roof and floor have been filled with sound-insulating material, and double windows with a small air space between have been provided, thereby reducing noise to a minimum.

All meals are prepared in two up-to-date all-electric kitchens. The electricity used for cooking, lighting, ventilating and refrigerating is supplied by axle-driven generators, the total power generated being 72 kilowatts.

* * *

New streamlined "Pacific" locomotives of the latest design have been constructed to haul, each in its turn, the "West Riding Limited."

The engines have been finished in Garter blue with stainless steel lettering and mouldings the wheels being coloured a dark red.

The leading dimensions are :—

Length over Buffers	71′ 0$\frac{3}{4}$″
Weight in working order	167 tons
Boiler Pressure	250 lb. per sq. in.
Diameter of Driving Wheels	6′ 8″
Cylinder Diameter	18$\frac{1}{2}$″
Stroke	26″
Tractive Effort	35,500 lb.

The corridor tender follows the general scheme of streamlining. It carries 8 tons of coal and 5,000 gallons of water.

* * *

The weight of a train alone is 278 tons, and its length over buffers 459′ 7$\frac{1}{2}$″. The weight with an engine attached is 445 tons, and the overall length 530′ 6$\frac{3}{4}$″.

9

BRADFORD LEEDS AND LONDON

FIG. 96

AUTHOR'S COLLECTION

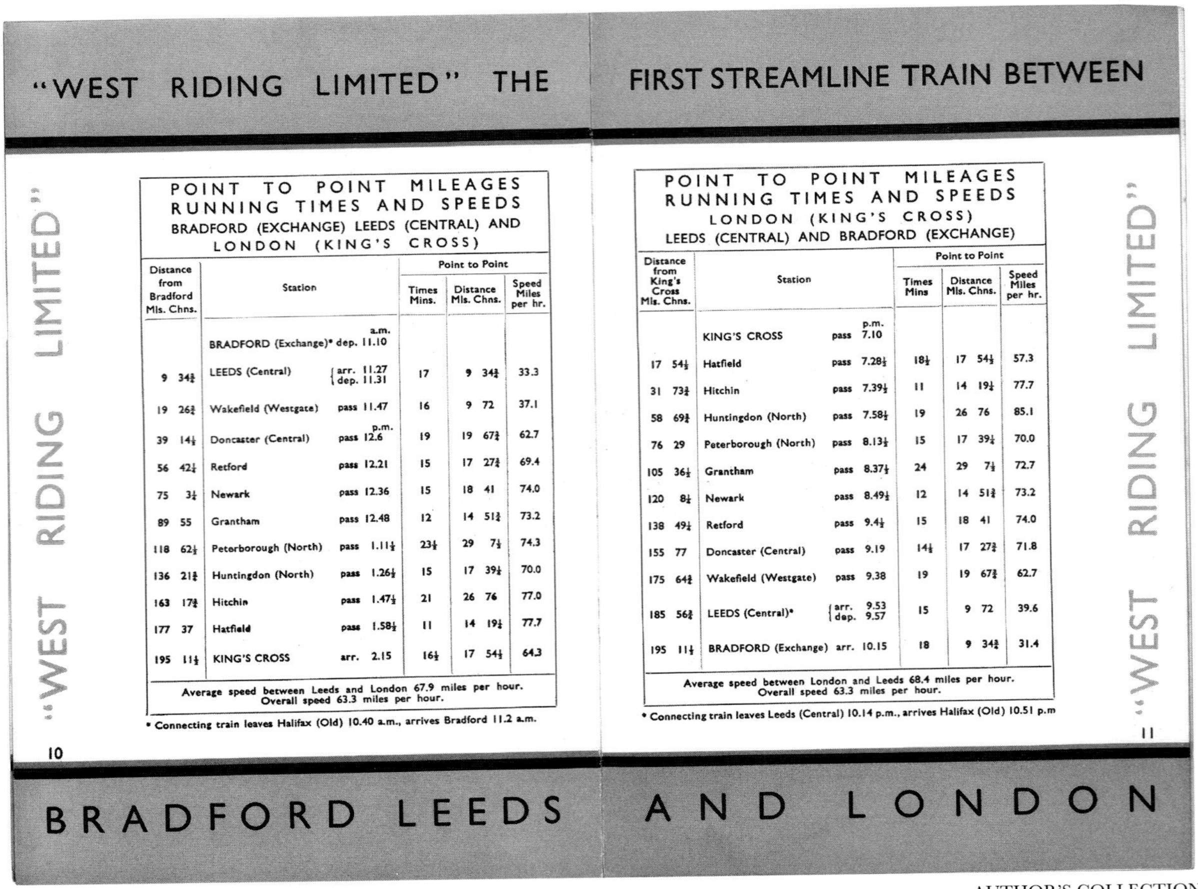

"WEST RIDING LIMITED" THE FIRST STREAMLINE TRAIN BETWEEN

"WEST RIDING LIMITED"

POINT TO POINT MILEAGES
RUNNING TIMES AND SPEEDS
BRADFORD (EXCHANGE) LEEDS (CENTRAL) AND
LONDON (KING'S CROSS)

Distance from Bradford Mls. Chns.	Station		Point to Point		
			Times Mins.	Distance Mls. Chns.	Speed Miles per hr.
	BRADFORD (Exchange)*	dep. a.m. 11.10			
9 34¾	LEEDS (Central)	arr. 11.27 / dep. 11.31	17	9 34¾	33.3
19 26¾	Wakefield (Westgate)	pass 11.47	16	9 72	37.1
39 14½	Doncaster (Central)	pass p.m. 12.6	19	19 67¾	62.7
56 42¼	Retford	pass 12.21	15	17 27¾	69.4
75 3¼	Newark	pass 12.36	15	18 41	74.0
89 55	Grantham	pass 12.48	12	14 51¾	73.2
118 62½	Peterborough (North)	pass 1.11½	23½	29 7½	74.3
136 21¾	Huntingdon (North)	pass 1.26½	15	17 39¼	70.0
163 17¾	Hitchin	pass 1.47½	21	26 76	77.0
177 37	Hatfield	pass 1.58½	11	14 19¼	77.7
195 11½	KING'S CROSS	arr. 2.15	16½	17 54½	64.3

Average speed between Leeds and London 67.9 miles per hour.
Overall speed 63.3 miles per hour.

* Connecting train leaves Halifax (Old) 10.40 a.m., arrives Bradford 11.2 a.m.

10

POINT TO POINT MILEAGES
RUNNING TIMES AND SPEEDS
LONDON (KING'S CROSS)
LEEDS (CENTRAL) AND BRADFORD (EXCHANGE)

Distance from King's Cross Mls. Chns.	Station		Point to Point		
			Times Mins	Distance Mls. Chns.	Speed Miles per hr.
	KING'S CROSS	pass p.m. 7.10			
17 54½	Hatfield	pass 7.28½	18½	17 54½	57.3
31 73¾	Hitchin	pass 7.39½	11	14 19¼	77.7
58 69¾	Huntingdon (North)	pass 7.58½	19	26 76	85.1
76 29	Peterborough (North)	pass 8.13½	15	17 39¼	70.0
105 36½	Grantham	pass 8.37½	24	29 7½	72.7
120 8¼	Newark	pass 8.49½	12	14 51¾	73.2
138 49¼	Retford	pass 9.4½	15	18 41	74.0
155 77	Doncaster (Central)	pass 9.19	14½	17 27¾	71.8
175 64¾	Wakefield (Westgate)	pass 9.38	19	19 67¾	62.7
185 56¾	LEEDS (Central)*	arr. 9.53 / dep. 9.57	15	9 72	39.6
195 11½	BRADFORD (Exchange)	arr. 10.15	18	9 34¾	31.4

Average speed between London and Leeds 68.4 miles per hour.
Overall speed 63.3 miles per hour.

* Connecting train leaves Leeds (Central) 10.14 p.m., arrives Halifax (Old) 10.51 p.m

"WEST RIDING LIMITED"

11

BRADFORD LEEDS AND LONDON

FIG. 97

AUTHOR'S COLLECTION

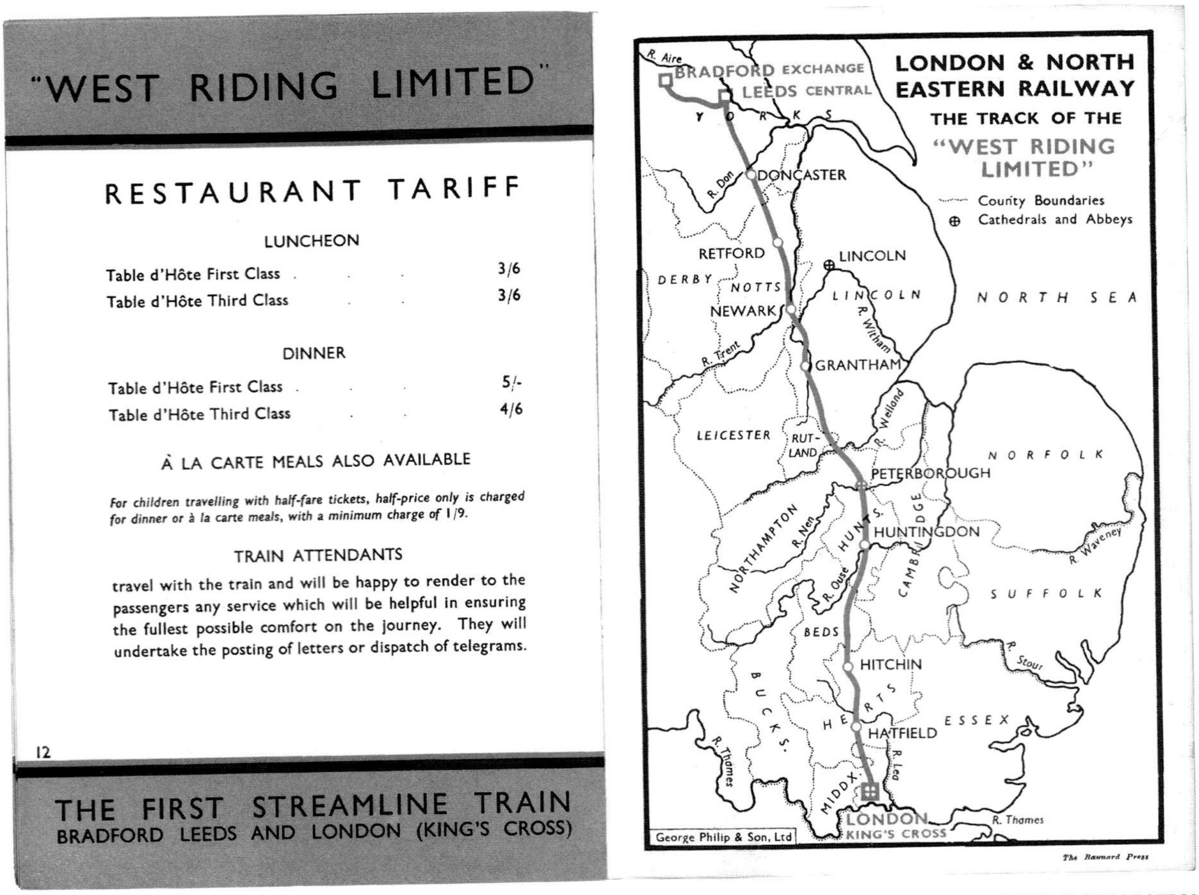

"WEST RIDING LIMITED"

RESTAURANT TARIFF

LUNCHEON

Table d'Hôte First Class	3/6
Table d'Hôte Third Class	3/6

DINNER

Table d'Hôte First Class	5/-
Table d'Hôte Third Class	4/6

À LA CARTE MEALS ALSO AVAILABLE

For children travelling with half-fare tickets, half-price only is charged for dinner or à la carte meals, with a minimum charge of 1/9.

TRAIN ATTENDANTS

travel with the train and will be happy to render to the passengers any service which will be helpful in ensuring the fullest possible comfort on the journey. They will undertake the posting of letters or dispatch of telegrams.

12

THE FIRST STREAMLINE TRAIN
BRADFORD LEEDS AND LONDON (KING'S CROSS)

LONDON & NORTH EASTERN RAILWAY
THE TRACK OF THE "WEST RIDING LIMITED"
County Boundaries
Cathedrals and Abbeys
R. Aire
BRADFORD EXCHANGE
LEEDS CENTRAL
YORKS
R. Don
DONCASTER
RETFORD
LINCOLN
DERBY
NOTTS
LINCOLN
NEWARK
R. Witham
NORTH SEA
R. Trent
GRANTHAM
R. Welland
LEICESTER
RUT-LAND
NORFOLK
PETERBOROUGH
NORTHAMPTON
R. Nen
HUNTS.
CAMBRIDGE
HUNTINGDON
R. Waveney
R. Ouse
SUFFOLK
BEDS
R. Stour
HITCHIN
BUCKS.
HERTS
ESSEX
HATFIELD
R. Thames
R. Lea
MIDDX.
LONDON
KING'S CROSS
R. Thames
George Philip & Son, Ltd
The Baynard Press

FIG. 98

AUTHOR'S COLLECTION

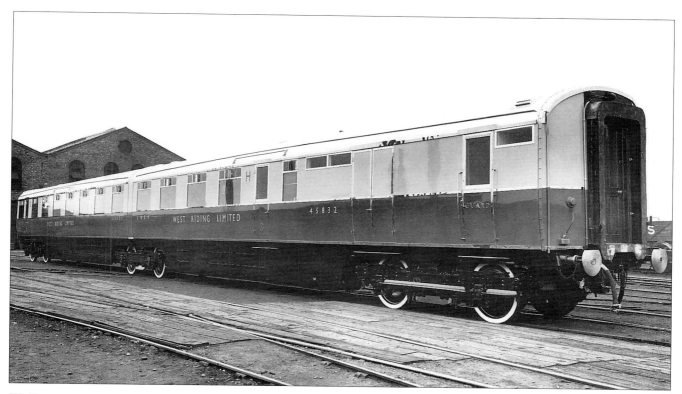

FIG. 99

DON 37/132

'West Riding Limited' articulated twin Third-class brake end No. 45832 with 45831 just out of the carriage shops in February 1937 and finished, like the 'Coronation' sets, in Marlborough Blue above the waistline and Garter Blue beneath. All strips, letters and numerals were in stainless steel. Introduced on Monday 27 September 1937, this was the third streamlined train to be put into service by the company and was primarily intended to enable the Bradford wool merchants to attend auctions held at the London Wool Exchange and return home the same day.

FIG. 100

DON 37/165

No. 4497 *Golden Plover*, Works No. 1862, built in October 1937 and put to work before she had left the confines of the Plant yard, albeit only to pose in front of the new Pilkington Glass Company's exhibition train before departing for her home shed at Haymarket. She was withdrawn as BR No. 60031 in October 1965.

FATAL ACCIDENT ON WISKE MOOR ON 8 OCTOBER 1937

The full Ministry of Transport accident report is reproduced by kind permission of the Railway Inspectorate, with photographs (from the Author's collection) taken during the subsequent enquiry.

FATAL ACCIDENT WHEN PICKING UP WATER ON WISKE MOOR WATER TROUGHS

SIR,

I have the honour to report for the information of the Minister of Transport, in accordance with the Order of the 21st October, 1937, the result of my Inquiry into the circumstances attending the fatal accident which occurred on the 8th October, 1937, to C. E. Skinner, between Danby Wiske and Northallerton, on the London and North Eastern Railway.

Skinner was employed as a Locomotive Inspector and was travelling on the engine of the southbound Coronation train which left Edinburgh at 4.30 p.m. The train passed the corresponding northbound train at about 7.27 p.m. when both engines were taking water at the Wiske Moor troughs, situated between Danby Wiske and Northallerton Stations. Skinner was standing on the right, or "sixfoot", side of the cab, watching the water gauge on the front of the tender, when a volume of water overflowed from the tender of the engine on the opposite track. Both trains were travelling at slightly over 70 miles an hour and the impact of the water broke the spectacle glass of the engine of the up train, to which Skinner had his back turned at the time. A portion of the glass was forced out of the lower corner of the frame and struck Skinner on the back of the head, inflicting injuries to which he succumbed almost immediately. The glass sight screen on the same side of the engine cab was also broken and, on the up train, a number of ventilator vanes, and two sliding ventilator lights were damaged. Apparently some of the damaged material came in contact with the down train, as a window drop light, and ventilator, of the leading coach were broken at the same time.

The engines of the southbound and northbound trains were Nos. 4492 and 4491 respectively. They were of the Dominion, 4-6-2, streamlined class, constructed in June of last year. The front windows of the cabs of these engines are set at an angle of $47\frac{1}{2}°$ to the longitudinal centre line of the engine and, together with the sight screens, are fitted with a type of safety glass designed to prevent splinters flying in the event of fracture.

The taking of water by the southbound train had no bearing on the accident, except that it explains Skinner's position, with his back turned in the direction of travel.

The northbound train was in charge of Driver William Hastie, and Locomotive Inspector Charles Conyers was travelling on the engine, with instructions to pay special attention to the picking up of water. Difficulty was being experienced at the time in obtaining sufficient water at certain troughs, and on the previous occasion when Hastie worked his train, two nights before the accident, he did not pick up sufficient water at Wiske Moor to take him to the next trough at Lucker, a distance of nearly 100 miles, with the result that he was compelled to make a special stop at Newcastle. Consequently the men on the footplate were intent on filling the tank as far as possible at Wiske Moor on this occasion.

The total water capacity of the tender is 5,000 gallons, and after taking as much water as time permitted during the three-minute stop at York, the engine ran on to the trough at Wiske Moor, 32 miles further north, with about 3,000 gallons in the tank. This figure is only approximate as it has to be gauged from a vertical test pipe on the front of the tender, with perforations at 6 ins. intervals. Hastie had the scoop lowered immediately to its full extent, and when he estimated from the gauge that the tank was nearly full, before the engine reached the end of the trough, he called to his fireman to lift the scoop. The fireman was unable to move it, and a considerable volume of water overflowed from the manhole and air vents at the top of the tender, with the results already described.

The scoop was examined on arrival at Edinburgh and was found to be at the correct height, and in good working order. It is lowered and raised by a screw, operated by a handle, which is similar in design and action to that of the tender hand brake. When it is in its lowest position for taking water, 3 or 4 turns of the handle are required to raise it clear of the water in the trough.

Owing to the resistance of the water when an engine is travelling at a high rate of speed, difficulty is sometimes experienced in raising the scoop if it is fully lowered. The practice is, therefore, either to dip the scoop partially from the commencement of the trough, in order to keep it under control, or to lower it fully when the engine has traversed part of the trough, so that, if necessary, it can be left in the water until it is automatically lifted out at the end, by the rise in the track, after which it can be raised to the running position without difficulty.

As an engine travelling at 70 miles an hour passes over a trough of 623 yards in length, as at Wiske Moor, in 18 seconds, the manipulation of the scoop requires considerable judgment, especially as the men can never be sure that a trough is full. The distances between the available points for obtaining water on a journey, either by trough or column, decides the amount of water which has to be taken at each trough and has an important bearing on the manipulation of the scoop. In this instance for example the northbound train was booked to travel without a stop from York to Edinburgh. It was of importance, therefore, that as much water as possible should be taken at Wiske Moor, having regard for the distance to the next trough at Lucker.

I am satisfied that reasonable care was exercised by all concerned and the accident may be attributed to misadventure.

It draws attention to the difficulties of taking water at high speeds and also the serious effects that an overflow from a tender may have upon a passing train in such conditions.

All the men whom I have had an opportunity of questioning appear to be fully aware of the importance of avoiding an overflow, as far as possible, but they are equally mindful of the consequences of failing to obtain a sufficient supply of water at a trough, when working a train with such brief stops. The latter consideration is of special importance to the north of York, where there are only two sets of water troughs between York and Edinburgh, whereas between London and York four sets of troughs are available in a slightly less distance.

In order to guard against an overflow I feel that the men should be provided with an easier means of working the scoop, whereby they will have absolute control over it in all conditions. They also need, in my opinion, a more sensitive water gauge on the tender, which will give them a better indication of the conditions within the tank, during the picking up of water. The present spacing of the water troughs is a further point for consideration; and as the risk of overflowing the tank cannot, even so, be entirely eliminated, I recommend that a stronger type of safety glass, which is better suited to withstand the impact of a volume of water or other objects at high speed, be fitted to the front windows and sight screens of engine cabs.

I would also suggest that the last mentioned recommendation be brought to the notice of the Railway Companies generally.

I have, etc.,

J. L. M. MOORE.

Author's note: Both engines involved in this accident were carrying locomotive inspectors supervising the picking up of water from the Wiske Moor troughs as engine crews had made complaints that insufficient water was being picked up at speed, with the result that the northbound train was often having to make an unscheduled stop at Newcastle to take on water.

FIG. 101

AUTHOR'S COLLECTION

No. 4497 *Golden Plover*, the engine used for the inquiry conducted by the Ministry of Transport inspector J. L. M. Moore. Running light engine over Scrooby troughs, selected for the trials, her tender tank is being allowed to overflow to gauge the effect this would have on a passing train. It is believed that these photographs were taken unofficially, hence their poor quality.

FIG. 102   AUTHOR'S COLLECTION

The same run over the troughs but photographed from the opposite side of the line. As a result of this accident the Triplex glass fitted to the A4's cab windows was replaced with a heavier armour-plated glass.

FIG. 103   AUTHOR'S COLECTION

No. 4497 coming to the end of Scrooby troughs. The fireman has raised the scoop and only light spray is evident.

FIG. 104

AUTHOR'S COLLECTION

No. 4497 on the test train with a flat truck between the tender and the engineer's saloon so that a clearer view of the overflow can be seen through the front windows of the saloon.

FIG. 105

AUTHOR'S COLLECTION

The water turbulence caused by the tender overflowing as seen by the Inspecting Officer from the front of the engineer's saloon. For reasons of stability, the intermediate flat truck is heavily weighed down with bars of pig iron. It would be very interesting to know the function of the box-like fitting on the top left hand of the tender back.

FIG. 106   DON 37/184

A4 No. 4498 *Sir Nigel Gresley*, Works No. 1863, built in November 1937 and allocated to King's Cross. This photograph was taken in early November 1937 when she was just out of the paint shop.

FIG. 107   DON 38/312 (12x10)

On 26 November 1937 No. 4498 was taken over to Marylebone station by driver Bill Samwells and fireman Harry Gray, where Mr William Whitelaw, Chairman of the company, accompanied by fellow directors and railway officers unveiled the nameplates, *Sir Nigel Gresley* on the 100th Pacific (designed by him), and presented Sir Nigel with a silver replica of his engine. Amongst those present were Bert Spencer, Sir Nigel's Chief Technical Assistant, R. A. Thom, Mechanical Engineer at Doncaster, O. V. S. Bulleid from the Southern Railway, who had only left Sir Nigel as his assistant on the first of the previous month, F. H. Eggleshaw, Works Manager, Doncaster and Edward Thompson, Mechanical Engineer, Darlington. Altogether a party of some twenty colleagues. In February 1938 the locomotive went back into the Plant to be repainted prior to attending an exhibition at Manchester. Having returned to Top Shed in spotless condition, the opportunity was taken to pose Sir Nigel alongside his engine for a photograph (above) which was taken in March 1938. In November 1938 she was returned to the Plant for a general repair, and on emergence on 16 January 1939 a number of detail changes could be seen. Gone were her cast brass nameplates, and instead there were individual Staybrite stainless steel letters and border screwed on to a brass backing plate which was finished with a bright red background; stainless steel letters and numerals instead of her previous gold shaded in red transfers. A chromium-plated whistle completed the new appearance. She was withdrawn as BR No. 60007 in February 1966 and sold to the A4 Preservation Society the following May.

FIG. 108

DON 41/90

A4 No. 4903 *Peregrine*, Works No. 1877, built in July 1938 and allocated to Doncaster shed. She was the last engine of the class of 35 built between 1935 and 1938, and was reputed to be the only A4 never to have hauled a streamlined train. Four A4s were built new with double chimneys, the first being *Mallard*, along with *Capercaillie*, *Seagull* and *Peregrine*. Photographed at the Plant on Thursday 2 October 1941. She was withdrawn as BR No. 60034 in August 1966.

FIG. 109

DON 43/3

B1 No. 8301 *Springbok*, built at Darlington in December 1942 and initially allocated to Darlington shed. She was the first engine of a class that was eventually to number 410 engines built by Darlington, The North British Locomotive Company and the Vulcan Foundry. Photographed in wartime livery of unlined black on Monday 18 January 1943. She was withdrawn as BR No. 61000 in March 1962.

DON 46/24

FIG. 110

Cab view of B1 *Springbok* now carrying the number 1000. Photograph taken on Friday 12 April 1946.

AUTHOR'S COLLECTION

FIG. 111

B1 No. 1237 *Geoffrey H. Kitson*, Works No. 26138, built by The North British Locomotive Company in September 1947 and allocated to Neville Hill, Leeds. This photograph was taken by the Darlington Drawing Office on Thursday 19 February 1948. The locomotive was withdrawn as BR No. 61237 in December 1966.

FIG. 112   DON 47/208

B1 No. 1249 *Fitzherbert Wright*, built by The North British Locomotive Company, Works No. 26150, in October 1947 and allocated to Doncaster shed. On the eve of nationalisation the company owned 274 engines of this class and decided that 18 of them should be named after directors of the company. This photograph was taken on Monday 15 December 1947 to show her fitted with new nameplates. She was withdrawn as BR No. 61249 in June 1964.

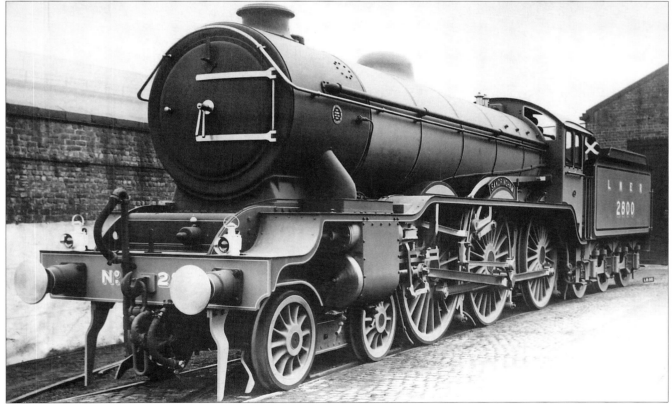

FIG. 113   AUTHOR'S COLLECTION

B17 No. 2800 *Sandringham*, built by The North British Locomotive Company, Works No. 23803, in December 1928 and allocated to Stratford. She was the first engine of her class and was photographed in grey prior to returning to the paint shop to receive her green livery. A total of 73 of her class were built by Darlington, The North British Locomotive Company and Robert Stephenson & Company, Newcastle. She was withdrawn as BR No. 61600 in July 1958.

FIG. 114   AUTHOR'S COLLECTION

B17 No. 2800 *Sandringham* (or so they would like you to think). The reverse side of this print states that this is really No. 2804, built by The North British Locomotive Company, Works No. 23807, in December 1928 and named *Elveden*. The reason for the deception was that the builders wanted a photograph of the first of the class for their official records. Why the real 2800 was not available is not known. She was allocated to Stratford before being sent on to Parkeston. She was withdrawn as BR No. 61604 in August 1953.

FIG. 115   DON 38/79

B17 No. 2805 *Lincolnshire Regiment*, built by The North British Locomotive Company, Works No. 23808, in December 1928 and allocated to Stratford, from where she was sent on to Parkeston a few weeks later. This photograph was taken in April 1938 after she had just undergone a general repair and had received her new nameplates. Up to this time she had been *Burnham Thorpe*. Fitted with a G.E.R. pattern tender and with both vacuum and Westinghouse brakes, she spent her working life on the Great Eastern section. She was withdrawn as BR No. 61605 in May 1958.

FIG. 116

L. HANSON

B17/2 No. 2818 *Wynard Park*, built at Darlington in November 1930 and allocated to Cambridge where this photograph was taken on Sunday 5 June 1932. She spent all of her working life on the Great Eastern section. Although she changed sheds on a number of occasions, she finished up where she had started at Cambridge, being withdrawn as BR No. 61618 in January 1960.

With ever an eye for publicity, the company selected two B17s, Nos. 2859 *Norwich City* and 2870 *Tottenham Hotspur*, and put them through the Plant from where they emerged in September 1937 complete with streamlined casings resembling two A4s and carrying the names *East Anglian* and *City of London* respectively. They were finished in the standard green and lined out in black and white.

These were to work the new 'East Anglian' service introduced on Monday 27 September which left Norwich at 11.55 a.m., arriving at Ipswich at 12.46 p.m., where a four-minute stop was allowed, arriving at Liverpool Street at 2.10 p.m. The return working left Liverpool Street at 6.40 p.m., arriving at Ipswich at 8 p.m. and Norwich at 8.55 p.m. Bearing in mind that the line speed was 80 mph, no advantage would be gained by providing two streamlined engines to work this train of six non-streamlined teak coaches.

The streamlining added in excess of three tons dead weight to each locomotive. With the 114 miles between Norwich and London being run at an average speed of 51 mph the thought must occur that the publicity department was involved in providing the service. However, one can imagine the effect on passengers waiting at stations en route for other services when suddenly one of the engines roared through the station, chime whistle blowing, followed by a train of immaculate teak coaches. The resultant publicity must have been enormous and well worth the capital outlay.

FIG. 117

DON 37/134

B17/5 No. 2859 *East Anglian*, built at Darlington in June 1936 and allocated to Gorton. When built she carried the name *Norwich City*, and was the first of the two engines picked for working the forthcoming 'East Anglian' service. In July 1937 she went into the Plant for a general repair, emerging in September having been streamlined in a similar manner to the A4s, but now named *East Anglian* and finished in the standard apple-green livery lined out in black edged in white. Upon leaving the Plant she proceeded to her new home at Norwich from where she worked the first 'East Anglian' to Liverpool Street on Monday 27 September 1937. In April 1951 her streamlining was removed. She was withdrawn as BR No. 61659 in March 1960.

FIG. 118   DON 37/138

B17/5 No. 2870 *City of London*, built by Robert Stephenson & Company, Works No. 4132, in May 1937 and allocated to Leicester. When she was built she carried the name *Manchester City*, but this was changed to *Tottenham Hotspur* in the same month. The following July she was the second engine chosen to work the forthcoming 'East Anglian' service. She was returned to the Plant from where she emerged in September in streamlined form and carrying the name *City of London*. The streamlining was eventually removed in 1951. She was withdrawn as BR No. 61670 in April 1960.

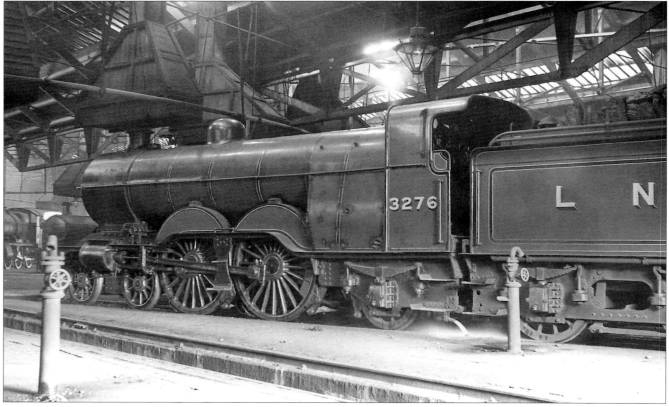

FIG. 119   L. HANSON

C1 No. 3276, Works No. 1034, built in June 1904 and allocated to Doncaster shed. When this photograph was taken on Sunday 18 October 1936 she had been transferred to Sheffield. Here she is seen away from home on shed at Swindon. She had worked into Swindon on the 9.15 a.m. from Sheffield via Woodford and Banbury before returning the next day. She was withdrawn in January 1946 still retaining her original LNER number.

FIG. 120

AUTHOR'S COLLECTION

C1 No. 3279, Works No. 1037, built in June 1904 and allocated to King's Cross. She was built as a standard two-cylinder engine, but in May 1915 Gresley rebuilt her as a four-cylinder simple engine with outside Walschaerts valve gear. The valves for the inside cylinders were driven by rocking levers connected to the outside valves. This photograph, taken in 1934, shows her on a down stopping train near Potters Bar. She was withdrawn as No. 2808 in February 1948 (see Figure 124).

FIG. 121

DON 38/98

Another view of No. 3279 (above), this time after being rebuilt again in 1938 back into a two-cylinder simple engine but retaining the outside Walschaerts valve gear. By now she had been reallocated to New England where she lived out the rest of her working life. She is photographed just out of the paint shop in June 1938. She was withdrawn as No. 2808 in February 1948.

FIG. 122

L. HANSON

C1 No. 3286, Works No. 1043, built in June 1904 and allocated to King's Cross. By the time this photograph was taken on Saturday 24 October 1936 she had been transferred to Hitchin shed. She is seen backing out of one of the arrival platforms at the Cross en route to the turntable before taking out a return working, probably back to Hitchin. She was withdrawn as LNER No. 2815 in October 1947.

FIG. 123

L. HANSON

C1s Nos. 3290 and 4401, Works Nos. 1048 and 1077, were built in June 1904 and June 1905 respectively. They were allocated to New England and Grantham and were still at those sheds when this photograph was taken of them on Saturday 27 June 1936 approaching Sandy on an up express. These engines were the mainstay of the company for working their fast traffic until the Pacifics were available in quantity. In later years they were usually double-headed when called upon to work heavy trains and had no trouble in keeping time. No. 3290 was withdrawn in November 1945 and No. 4401 was withdrawn as LNER No. 2831 in November 1946.

FIG. 124

L. HANSON

C1 No. 3301, Works No. 1074, built in May 1905 and allocated to King's Cross where she remained until 1941. In this view she is approaching Sandy on an up express on Saturday 1 May 1937. She was withdrawn as LNER No. 2829 in July 1948.

FIG. 125

AUTHOR'S COLLECTION

C1 No. 4413, Works No. 1111, built in March 1906 and allocated to New England. Photographed in the Plant in the late 1920s. Possibly at the time she was undergoing a general repair and the fitting of a 32-element superheater in July 1929. Filling and rubbing down seems to be taking place prior to her entry into the paint shop. She was withdrawn in January 1946.

FIG. 126   DON 23/10

C1 No. 1415, Works No. 1113, built in April 1906 and allocated to Grantham where she was to remain until 1944.
Photographed on the Plant turntable on Friday 27 April 1923 still carrying her GNR number which she retained until July
1925 when she became No. 4415 (all GN engines had 3000 added to their numbers at the amalgamation). No. 4415 was
withdrawn as No. 2845 in April 1947. In the background is St James's Church which was built in May 1857 on land given
by the GNR. At the time, a majority of shareholders had refused to sanction funds to cover the cost of building the church,
much to the disgust of the Chairman of GNR, Edmund Denison. However, Denison was determined that his nearly 1,000-
strong workforce should have their place of worship, so he opened a subscription list amongst his friends and sympathetic
shareholders, raising enough to finance the project.

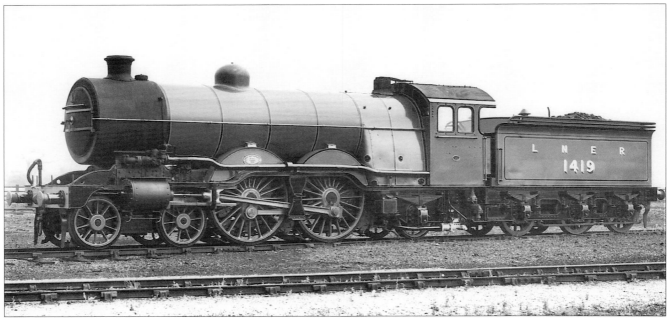

FIG. 127   DON 23/38

C1 No. 1419 (later 4419). See also Figure 128 opposite.

C1 No. 1419 (later 4419), Works No. 1117, built in May 1906 and allocated to Doncaster shed where she remained until 1924. In 1923 she entered the Plant Works for a general repair and was rebuilt with an American booster driving on the rear trailing wheels and with a superheated boiler. This was done to enable trials to be carried out to see whether it would help the engine in starting heavy trains. There were no problems with their steaming capabilities, with their wide fire boxes, but the adhesion from the four coupled wheels made it very difficult to get the trains moving. The trials proved this to be a great help, enabling heavy trains to be started from the most difficult situations. These two photographs were taken on Wednesday 15 August 1923. When the booster was fitted, the frames of the engine had to be lengthened by 25 inches to accommodate it, and the cab had to be extended. The steam to the booster was carried through a pipe along the left-hand side of the boiler, exhausting through a pipe along the right-hand side leading to the smoke box. These, together with the side windows in the cab, gave her a very different appearance from other members of her class. During another general repair in 1935 the booster was removed, although she retained her lengthened frames and cab. She was withdrawn as LNER No. 2849 in July 1948.

FIG. 128 · DON 23/40

FIG. 129 · L. HANSON

C1 No. 4426, Works No. 1151, built in May 1907 and allocated to Cambridge. In 1924 she was transferred to King's Cross where she spent the rest of her working life. This photograph was taken on Saturday 25 May 1935 and shows her working the down 'West Riding Pullman' having just cleared Sandy station. She was withdrawn in February 1944 when her boiler and fire box were considered beyond economical repair.

FIG. 130   L. HANSON

C1 No. 4434, Works No. 1173, built in November 1907 and allocated to Doncaster shed. In June 1923 she was moved on to Sheffield. This photograph was taken on Sunday 29 March 1936 and shows her on foreign territory at the Great Western shed at Banbury. She had probably come in on a Sunday working from Sheffield via Woodford. Having had her fire cleaned, taken on water and her crew rested, she would be ready to change places with the GWR engine that would have brought in her train, the 10.25 a.m. from Swansea. She was due out at 4.16 p.m. on her return working to Sheffield. She was withdrawn in April 1945.

FIG. 131   L. HANSON

C1 No. 4437, Works No. 1186, built in March 1908 and allocated to New England. Running light engine on the up slow waiting for a path through the Sandy station bottleneck (four roads down to two) on Saturday 1 May 1937. By this time she was a Hitchin engine and was probably returning home after working to Peterborough. If this was the case, I wonder why she was not turned on the triangle at New England. She was withdrawn in March 1944.

FIG. 132

L. HANSON

C1 No. 4439, Works No. 1188, built in March 1908 and allocated to New England. In 1933 she was transferred to Cambridge. Here at King's Cross she is awaiting the right away on the 11.30 p.m. for Cambridge on Sunday 10 November 1934. She was withdrawn as LNER No. 2869 in January 1947.

FIG. 133

L. HANSON

C1 No. 4440, Works No. 1189, built in April 1908 and allocated to King's Cross. By the time this photograph was taken at King's Cross on Tuesday 19 April 1938 she had been transferred to Cambridge. After working in to the Cross from Cambridge she is in company with N2 No. 2687 en route to the engine yard, where she will be turned and prepared before a return working to Cambridge. She was withdrawn as LNER No. 2870 in February 1948.

FIG. 134   L. HANSON

C1 No. 4452, Works No. 1276, built in August 1910 and allocated to Doncaster shed. Saturday 27 June 1936 sees her approaching Sandy with an up excursion of cream and green tourist stock. The company, with Bulleid very much involved, built five of these 12-coach trains. Each train consisted of six twin articulated plywood-bodied coaches instead of the more usual teak. They were built with economy in mind, in an attempt to attract passengers on to special excursions at a time when money was still very tight. They certainly created a holiday atmosphere when seen amidst the more sombre varnished teak coaches. The engine is carrying Reporting No. 17. She was withdrawn in February 1946.

FIG. 135   AUTHOR'S COLLECTION

C2 No. 3260, Works No. 1005, built in June 1903 and allocated to the GNR shed at York. Upon the amalgamation she moved to Doncaster shed. The photograph was taken at New England on Sunday 16 June 1935, by which time she had again been transferred this time to King's Cross. She was withdrawn in September 1936.

FIG. 136

Another photograph of C2 No. 3260 taken just over a year later on Saturday 27 June 1936. Drifting into Sandy on an up parly. A King's Cross engine at this time, she had just three more months of work in front of her before being withdrawn in September 1936.

FIG. 137

AUTHOR'S COLLECTION

C12 No. 1009A, Works No. 755, built in February 1898 and allocated to the West Riding. She was the first of her class which by July 1907 was to number 60 engines in total. Destination board brackets are fitted on the top half of the smoke box door. Bogie brakes were fitted in September 1912. In August 1921 she had the suffix 'A' added to her number so that the number 1009 could be used elsewhere. She became 4009A in 1926. This photograph would have been taken circa 1923. She was withdrawn as BR No. 67350 in April 1955.

FIG. 138   L. HANSON

C12 No. 4508, Works No. 819, built in May 1899. From engine No. 4502 the side tank ends were rounded. Compare this photograph with that of No. 1009A in Figure 137. This photograph was taken at New England on Sunday 16 June 1935. She was withdrawn as BR No. 67366 in April 1958.

FIG. 139   DON 39/123

D49/1 No. 234 *Yorkshire*, built at Darlington in October 1927 and allocated to York. In this view she is seen posed for her first-of-class official photograph, painted in photographic grey and lined out in black and white. Note the Darlington practice of painting the cylinder covers engine colour, whilst Doncaster always painted them black. This was a hangover from North Eastern Railway practice. She was withdrawn as BR No. 62700 in October 1958.

FIG. 140   AUTHOR'S COLLECTION

D49/1 No. 246 *Morayshire*, built at Darlington in February 1928 and allocated to Dundee. This photograph caught her on shed at Eastfield in 1929 still carrying the works plates on her cab sides with the running number on her tender. Being fitted with both vacuum and Westinghouse brakes, she carried an air pump on her right-hand running plate. She was withdrawn as BR No. 62712 in July 1961 and, after spending time as a stationary boiler, she was purchased for preservation by Ian Fraser of Arbroath in January 1965.

FIG. 141   L. HANSON

D49/1 No. 306 *Roxburghshire*, built at Darlington in March 1928 and allocated to St Margaret's. Here, on Thursday 4 August 1938, she is passing Princes Street Gardens with a fast train for Edinburgh Waverley. Despite their handsome appearance, they were most unpopular with their crews because of their rough riding characteristics. She was withdrawn as BR No. 62715 in June 1959.

FIG. 142   L. HANSON

D49/1 No. 2759 *Cumberland*, built at Darlington in May 1929 and allocated to Eastfield. This class of engine was Gresley's first design for the new LNER company and has been said to have been the least successful of his engines. Photographed on shed at Haymarket on Sunday 1 August 1937. She was withdrawn as BR No. 62734 in March 1961.

FIG. 143   AUTHOR'S COLLECTION

D49/1 No. 2760 *Westmorland*, built at Darlington in June 1929 and allocated to Eastfield where this photograph was taken later that year. Twenty-eight Part 1s were built with Walschaerts valve gear with piston valves, although this number was increased in 1938 when the six Part 3s were rebuilt to Part 1. She was withdrawn as BR No. 62735 in August 1958.

FIG. 144

L. HANSON

D49/2 No. 376 *The Staintondale*, built at Darlington in February 1935 and allocated to York. She was the penultimate engine out of a class of 42 built with Lentz rotary cam poppet valves. Twelve-spoke bogie wheels were fitted as a result of Darlington using their North-Eastern Railway patterns, as against the ten-spoke used at Doncaster. Photographed on shed at York on Saturday 30 June 1935. She was withdrawn as BR No. 62774 in November 1958.

FIG. 145

DON 47/13

D49/3 No. 318 *Cambridgeshire*, built at Darlington in May 1928 and allocated to Neville Hill. She was the first of a batch of six engines fitted with Lentz oscillating cam valve gear. All six were rebuilt to Part 1 with Walschaerts valve gear in 1938. This picture was taken at Darlington when she was new, the photograph being copied by Doncaster in 1947. She was withdrawn as BR No. 62720 in October 1959.

L. HANSON

FIG. 146

J1 No. 3003, Works No. 1203, built in September 1908. This photograph was taken on Saturday 1 May 1937, at which time she was a King's Cross engine. Leaving Sandy on a parly on the down fast line, she is getting under way. It was more usual for these trains to be put on the slow roads. They cannot have been very profitable for the company as the author knows from his own observation that the two coaches would contain less than a dozen passengers on many occasions. She was withdrawn as BR No. 65002 in August 1954. (A parly, or parliamentary, train was one run as a result of an act of 1844 which required that any company that derived a third of its income from passenger traffic was to run at least one train a day, including Sundays, in each direction calling at every station.)

L. HANSON

FIG. 147

J2 No. 3075, Works No. 1356, was built in September 1912. One of a class of ten engines, she is seen on shed at New England on Sunday 16 June 1935. The tender has been coaled up, her clinker thrown out and she stands ready for the steam raiser to do his job at the appointed hour. She was withdrawn as BR 65019 in March 1953.

FIG. 148

DON 29/130

J4 No. 4084, Works No. 705, built in October 1896. After undergoing a general repair she poses for her official photograph in October 1929. Still retaining her Stirling cab she was withdrawn in March 1933.

FIG. 149

L. HANSON

J5 No. 3036, Works No. 1252, built in December 1909. She was one of a class of 20 engines built for working coal traffic. Photographed on Sunday 16 June 1935, she is on shed at New England awaiting her next day's work. She was withdrawn as BR No. 65495 in August 1954.

FIG. 150   HOPKINS BROWN/JOHN CRAWLEY

J6 No. 522, Works No. 1312, built in September 1911. Photographed on shed at Colwick on Saturday 26 May 1923 still carrying her GN number (later to be 3522). In April 1916 she was fitted with a top feed water heater which incorporated a second dome ahead of the steam dome, both being enclosed in an elongated cover. This apparatus was removed in March 1923, although she carried the elongated cover until January 1931. She was withdrawn as BR No. 64171 in September 1961.

FIG. 151   AUTHOR'S COLLECTION

J6 No. 3537, Works No. 1363, built in November 1912. At the time of grouping she was a Manchester engine. This photograph, taken in 1935, shows her just having been coaled up at New England in 1935. She was withdrawn as BR No. 64186 in January 1958.

FIG. 152

L. HANSON

J38 No. 1417, built at Darlington in March 1926 and allocated to St Margaret's where she was to stay for the whole of her LNER life. Designed for working heavy goods traffic over the difficult lines in Scotland, all 35 engines of the class were allocated to the Scottish area. Photographed on shed at Eastfield on Tuesday 3 August 1937. She was withdrawn as BR No. 65915 in November 1966.

FIG. 153

DON 43/83

J39 No. 1448, built at Darlington in September 1926 and allocated to Newport. Designed as a mixed traffic engine, they had coupled wheels of 5 ft. 2 in. in diameter – 6 in. larger than the very similar engines of Class J38. She was the first engine of her class that was to number 289, the most prolific class of Gresley engines. They were the company's maid of all work, being used on anything from branch line duties to express passenger trains. Here she is posing for her first-of-class official photograph, grey paint lined out in white with certain of her fittings and coupling rods picked out in white. She was withdrawn as BR No. 64700 in April 1961.

FIG. 154 DON 29/78

J39 No. 2705, built at Darlington in September 1928 and allocated to Doncaster shed. After a short time she was sent to Mexborough, returning in April 1929 to Doncaster where this photograph was taken on Saturday 1 June 1929. She was withdrawn as BR No. 64758 in November 1962.

FIG. 155 L. HANSON

J39 No. 2731, built at Darlington in May 1929 and allocated to York. By the time this photograph was taken on Thursday 4 August 1932 she had been moved to Eastfield. She was withdrawn as BR No. 64784 in August 1960.

FIG. 156

AUTHOR'S COLLECTION

J39 No. 2962, built at Darlington in September 1931 and allocated to Gorton. From this engine onwards the class was fitted with a new form of operating mechanism for dropping the fire grate sections. Here she is seen posing for her official photograph, complete with a full set of lamps as was the Darlington practice on new engines. She was withdrawn as BR No. 64823 in January 1961.

FIG. 157

DON 26/29

J50/3 No. 610, Works No. 1648, built in August 1926 and allocated to Ardsley from where she was to spend most of her working life. Engines built from 1926 onwards were fitted with Ross pop safety valves in place of the Ramsbottom type fitted to all previously built J50s. Photographed on Thursday 1 July 1926 after emerging from the paint shop in photographic grey finish lined out in black and white. She entered traffic the following month after receiving her black workaday finish. She was withdrawn as BR No. 68951 in July 1961.

FIG. 158   DON 29/44

J50/3 No. 1082, Works No. 1667, built in April 1927. This photograph was taken at Immingham on Thursday 4 April 1929 for the Chief Mechanical Engineer's records. This engine was fitted with plain coupling rods. She was withdrawn as BR No. 68970 in April 1961.

FIG. 159   DON 29/167

J52 No. 3927, Works No. 608, built in April 1893 and fitted with condensing apparatus for working the London widened lines. Photographed at the Plant on Thursday 12 December 1929 after conversion from Class J53. She was withdrawn as BR No. 68761 in May 1957.

FIG. 160

L. HANSON

J52 No. 4051, built by Neilson & Company, Works No. 5022, in July 1896 and fitted with condensing gear. On the front is N2 No. 4613, Works No. 1528, built in August 1921 and also fitted with condensing gear. Seen in King's Cross about to remove empty stock on Monday evening 30 March 1937. They were withdrawn as BR Nos. 68788 and 69497 in December 1954 and March 1958 respectively.

FIG. 161

L. HANSON

J52 No. 4232, built by Sharp Stewart & Company, Works No. 4477, in April 1899. Allocated to King's Cross where she is seen on shunting duties on Saturday 12 August 1933. She was withdrawn as BR No. 68831 in January 1959.

FIG. 162   DON 37/10

K2 No. 4632, Works No. 1373, built in February 1913, originally as Class K1. At the time of the amalgamation in 1923 she was a King's Cross engine. She entered the Plant for rebuilding in October 1936. The company negative register records that this picture was taken on Friday 5 March 1937 to show her in rebuilt form. She was withdrawn as BR No. 61722 in September 1955.

FIG. 163   DON 31/98

K2 No. 4634, Works No. 1375, built in February 1913 and allocated to Ardsley. This photograph was taken on Wednesday 10 June 1931 after rebuilding from Class K1 to K2. She was withdrawn as BR No. 61724 in January 1958.

FIG. 164

L. HANSON

K2 No. 4659, Works No. 1475, built in December 1916. Photographed on a Class 'A' goods taking the down slow road just after passing through Sandy station on Saturday 1 May 1937. She was withdrawn as BR No. 61749 in January 1959.

FIG. 165

L. HANSON

K2 No. 4681, built by Kitson & Company in June 1921, Works No. 5331, and seen here approaching Sandy on the up fast line with a No. 2 goods on Saturday 1 May 1937. Judging by the amount of coal on the tender, she probably took over the train at Peterborough. She was withdrawn as BR No. 61771 in December 1960.

FIG. 166
AUTHOR'S COLLECTION

K2 No. 4683, built by Kitson & Company, Works No. 5333, in June 1921 and allocated to New England. Here she is heading a stopping train made up from a variety of interesting vehicles. The time and place were not recorded, but the date is thought to be circa 1927. She was withdrawn as BR No. 61773 in December 1960.

FIG. 167
AUTHOR'S COLLECTION

K2 No. 4688, built by Kitson & Company, Works No. 5338, in July 1921 and allocated to Doncaster shed. In March 1928 she was fitted with a Westinghouse pump and transferred over to the G.E. section where she is seen on a Liverpool Street to Clacton fast train circa 1930. She remained on the G.E. until after nationalisation. She was withdrawn as BR No. 61778 in October 1959.

FIG. 168

K3 No. 229, built at Darlington in October 1925 and allocated to Gorton, but had been moved to King's Cross when this photograph was taken on Saturday 1 May 1937, here waiting for a path through the Sandy station bottleneck with a train of fitted vans. She was withdrawn as BR No. 61868 in May 1962.

FIG. 169

K3 No. 2769, built at Darlington in August 1930 and allocated to Carlisle. In April 1932 she was transferred to Eastfield where this photograph was taken on Thursday 4 August 1932. She was withdrawn as BR No. 61898 in February 1959.

FIG. 170 DON 38/133

K3 No. 3816, built at Darlington in November 1936 and allocated to Doncaster shed. In this photograph, taken in October 1938, she is seen at the works after undergoing a general repair and being used for trials fitted with air raid precautionary anti-glare screens. After this she was returned to her shed at Gorton. She was withdrawn as BR No. 61976 in January 1962.

FIG. 171 DON 44/62

L1 No. 9000? No, this is V1 No. 2900 built up in a composite photograph to give an indication of what a proposed 2-6-4 tank engine would look like. The side tanks have been lengthened by painting them in, as has the rear bunker. The fitting of a four-wheel bogie adds to the illusion. This doctored photograph was produced by the Drawing Office and is dated Friday 31 March 1944. It makes an interesting comparison with the photograph in Figure 172 which shows this proposed engine as it was when built.

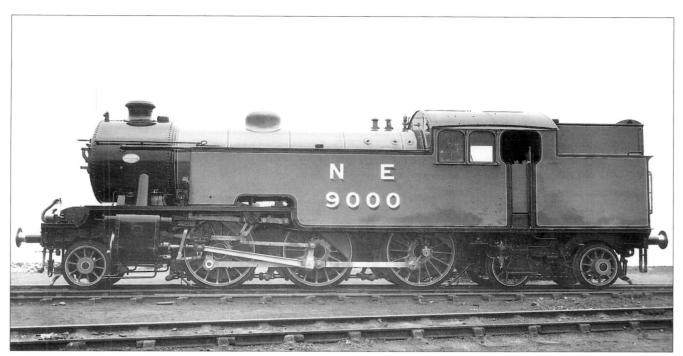

FIG. 172 DON 45/85

L1 No. 9000, Works No. 1984, built in May 1945 and allocated to Stratford. The first engine of a class of 100 and the only one to be built at Doncaster. Photographed in LNER livery of green, lined out in black and white, making her debut from the paint shop on Tuesday 22 May 1945. The other 99 came out under the auspices of British Railways, 29 being built at Darlington, and 35 each at the North British Locomotive Co. and Robert Stephenson & Hawthorns. She was withdrawn as BR No. 67701 in December 1960.

FIG. 173 DON 45/87

This photograph shows the Westinghouse pump on the right-hand running plate for working engine and train brakes. Destination board brackets are fitted on the smoke box door. The protrusion on the top of the smoke box is the daytime hinged indicator disc in the down (no show) position.

FIG. 174   DON 45/91

On Tuesday 29 May 1945 she ran light engine to King's Cross top shed where she was checked over, possibly being inspected by members of the Locomotive Committee, before being sent on to Stratford shed on 6 June, from where she carried out extensive trials on the G. E. section. After these had been completed, she carried out similar trials in the various regions. She was something of a nomad, staying at 23 sheds during her working life of 15½ years. She was the first engine to be fitted with electric lighting, the current being provided by an alternator fitted to the end of the near-side rear bogie axle. Later these had a propensity for dropping off, so were replaced by a Stones steam-driven generator fitted on the front end of the right-hand running plate.

FIG. 175   DON 45/89

Inside the cab of No. 9000.

FIG. 176   DON 33/78

N1 No. 4551, Works No. 1176, built in December 1907. In this view, photographed on Thursday 21 September 1933, she is seen on the Plant locomotive weighing machine table. She was withdrawn as BR No. 69431 in March 1955.

FIG. 177   L. HANSON

N1 No. 4602, Works No. 1347, built in June 1912 and fitted with condensing gear. In March 1924 she received a Robinson superheater together with twin pepper-pot anti-vacuum valves behind the chimney. Photographed at King's Cross on Tuesday 19 April 1938. She was withdrawn as BR No. 69482 in August 1954.

FIG. 178   L. HANSON

N2/1 No. 4741, built by the North British Locomotive Company, Works No. 22597, in February 1921 and allocated to King's Cross. Fitted with condensing gear, she was able to work the Metropolitan widened lines when required. Photographed at King's Cross on Saturday 24 October 1936 awaiting her next turn of duty which, from the relaxed posture of the fireman, was not imminent. She was withdrawn as BR No. 69520 in September 1962.

FIG. 179   L. HANSON

N2/1 No. 4770, built by the North British Locomotive Company, Works No. 22626, in April 1921 and allocated to King's Cross. Fitted with condensing gear, she too was able to work the Metropolitan widened lines. In this photograph, taken at King's Cross on Tuesday 2 April 1934, she is carrying a High Barnet destination board, although she is not standing in a platform road. These engines were the mainstay of the suburban services, working not only down the Drain, as the widened lines were known, but also covering most of the north London branch lines. She was withdrawn as BR No. 69549 in September 1961.

FIG. 180

L. HANSON

N2/1 No. 4611, Works No. 1525, built in July 1921 fitted with condensing gear, and allocated to King's Cross. Having brought in empty stock to form a northbound train which has since departed, she has been released to the end of the platform starting signal where she was photographed waiting for the road on Tuesday evening 30 March 1937. She was withdrawn as BR No. 69495 in September 1958.

FIG. 181

DON 25/91

N2/3 No. 897, Works No. 1632, built in December 1925 and allocated to Scotland. She had both vacuum and Westinghouse brakes. Here, on Thursday 10 December 1925, she has been pulled out of the paint shop for her official photograph. She entered traffic early in 1926 after returning to the paint shop for her workaday finish. She was withdrawn as BR No. 69567 in April 1959.

FIG. 182   DON 28/117

N2/4 No. 2682, built by the Yorkshire Engine Co. Limited, Works No. 2220, in September 1928. She was the first of nine engines supplied by this company, the first three of which were fitted with condensing gear, vacuum brakes and left-hand drive. This photograph was taken on Thursday 27 September 1928 for record purposes the day before she entered traffic. She was withdrawn as BR No. 69588 in February 1960.

FIG. 183   DON 26/20

O1 No. 3476, built by the North British Locomotive Company, Works No. 22103, in November 1919 and allocated to New England. This photograph was taken on Thursday 17 June 1926, when she was in the Plant for a general repair, possibly for record purposes to show the Worthington feed water heater and pump which had been fitted in 1922. These were removed in 1937 and she was withdrawn as LNER No. 3494 in March 1948.

FIG. 184   DON 26/21

A close-up view of the Worthington feed water heater and vertical pump as fitted to O1 No. 3476 (see Figure 183).

FIG. 185   DON 42/112

O2/3 No. 3844, Works No. 1942, built in 1942 and allocated to Doncaster shed. This interesting detail photograph was taken on Friday 23 October 1942. She was withdrawn as BR No. 63974 in September 1963.

FIG. 186   L. HANSON

O2/2 No. 3494, Works No. 1581, built in December 1923 and allocated to New England. Here photographed at Sandy on Saturday 1 May 1937 on a Class 'D' down stopping goods, having probably just picked up wagons from the Sandy goods yard, hence the effort in getting her train under way. She was withdrawn as BR No. 63939 in September 1963.

FIG. 187 DON 26/53

O2/2 No. 3495, Works No. 1582, built in February 1924 and allocated to New England. This engine was one of a batch of 15 ordered after the 1923 amalgamation to comply with the new loading gauge. This was necessary to cover the pregrouping companies which had been absorbed into the newly formed LNER. The photograph, taken on Wednesday 15 September 1926, shows the altered profile of the cab and the shorter chimney. She was withdrawn as BR No. 63940 in September 1963.

FIG. 188 L. HANSON

O2/2 No. 3496, Works No. 1584, built in February 1924 and allocated to Doncaster shed, although by the time this photograph was taken on Saturday 27 June 1936 she had been moved to New England. Having just come through Sandy station, she has just been put into the slow road with a Class 'A' goods. She was withdrawn as BR No. 63941 in September 1963.

FIG. 189

DON 25/8

O2/2 No. 3500, Works No. 1594, built in May 1924 and allocated to New England. Photographed on Tuesday 27 January 1925, it shows the Dabeg feed water heater which had just been fitted. Water was taken from the tender and heated by exhaust steam before being pumped into the boiler. This equipment was removed in December 1942. She was withdrawn as BR No. 63945 in September 1963.

FIG. 190

DON 25/9

A close-up view of the Dabeg feed water heater and horizontal tandem pump as fitted on O2/2 No. 3500.

FIG. 191   DON 25/45

Soon after the amalgamation in 1923 Gresley had in mind a heavy goods engine that would be able to relieve the build up of loaded coal wagons in the New England sidings awaiting forwarding to the Ferme Park sidings in London. His standard Class 02, 2-8-0s were doing splendid work but he wanted something even more powerful that could cope with bigger loads. After much deliberation two Class P1 2-8-2s were built. In this photograph taken on Wednesday 6 May 1925 engine No. 2394 is seen under construction at Doncaster. Cylinders, slide bars and smoke box saddle are in position, whilst the running plate framing is taking shape.

FIG. 192   AUTHOR'S COLLECTION

Another photograph of P1 2394 taken shortly after the previous one. Most of the running plate has now been fitted, as have the front buffers. In the background can be seen the first engine of the class, No. 2393, nearing completion.

FIG. 193 (ABOVE)   AUTHOR'S COLLECTION

The booster for No. 2394 posed for an official photograph. Supplied by the Locomotive Booster Company of Baltimore, USA, it was provided with two cylinders of 10-inch diameter with a stroke of 12 inches. The booster was removed from 2394 in April 1937, whilst 2393 retained hers until May 1938, albeit with many modifications.

FIG. 194 (LEFT)   AUTHOR'S COLLECTION

The booster now in position. The steam inlet pipe comes in on the far side, whilst the exhaust is led along the right-hand side of the engine to the smoke box. The steam pipes between the floating booster and the engine were a source of trouble. Although fitted with articulated couplings, the connecting pipes were continually breaking.

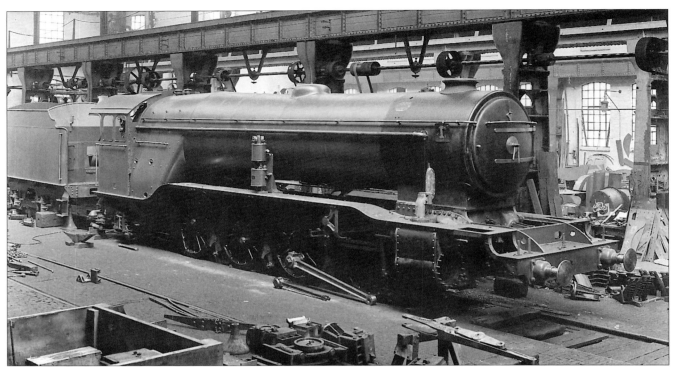

FIG. 195 AUTHOR'S COLLECTION

P1 No. 2393 nears completion in the Doncaster assembly shop in May 1925. The Westinghouse compressor mounted on the running plate provided air for engaging or disengaging the booster drive. The booster exhaust pipe can be seen entering the smoke box just above the running plate. She appears to have been undercoated as work proceeded.

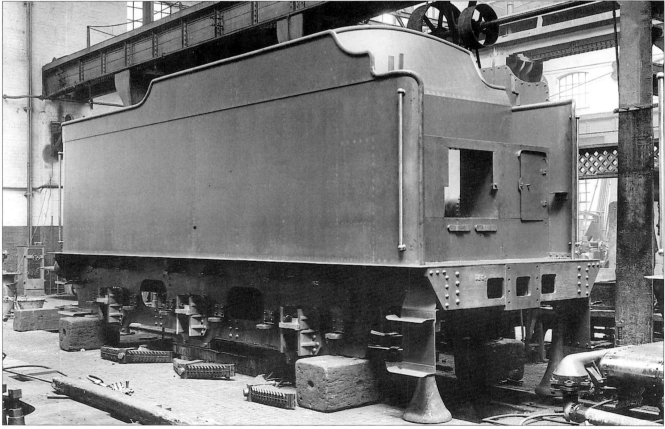

FIG. 196 AUTHOR'S COLLECTION

Tender No. 5293 had a water capacity of 4,700 gallons and could carry seven tons of coal. This photograph, which is a close-up of the above illustration, shows her well on the way to completion. The springs are lying alongside ready for fitting once the tender is lifted to receive her wheels and axle boxes.

FIG. 197

DON 25/65

P1 No. 2393, Works No. 1619, built in June 1925 and allocated to Doncaster shed for just over a month, no doubt to enable the Plant to keep an eye on her in the event of any teething troubles. She was then sent to New England where she was to spend her working life. There were no problems with her capacity for hauling long trains, and 100-wagon coal trains became the order of the day. The practical experience gained from the working of these trains soon showed up the flaws in the concept. When working they occupied three block sections and upon arrival at Ferme Park they had to occupy a running line until the train could be split up into more manageable lengths. This caused considerable problems for the Operating Department and was the eventual reason why they resorted to running the 70- to 80-wagon trains in which the two P1s still played their part. Photographed prior to entering traffic on Saturday 25 July 1925. She was withdrawn in July 1945.

FIG. 198

DON 26/15

P1 No. 2394, Works No. 1620, built in November 1925 and, like her sister, first went to Doncaster shed before moving on to New England after a suitable probationary period. Originally she differed from 2393 in having twin pepper-pot anti-vacuum valves behind the chimney. With a change of superheater, these were removed in November 1931, a single mushroom-type taking their place. The steam supply to the booster can be seen running from the smoke box saddle inside the frames and thence emerging under the cab side to the booster. Photographed on Monday 14 June 1926. She was withdrawn in July 1945.

FIG. 199

Early in 1932 planning began to build an eight-coupled engine to work the very difficult Edinburgh to Aberdeen road which abounded in sharp curves and heavy gradients. The first engine of Class P2/1, as they were to be called, was No. 2001 *Cock o' the North* and this photograph, taken in March 1934 at Doncaster Plant, shows her main frames being cut out of 1⅛ inch thick steel plate with an oxy-acetylene burner.

FIG. 200 DON 34/26

No. 2001's frame plates in the slotting machine at the Plant in March 1934.

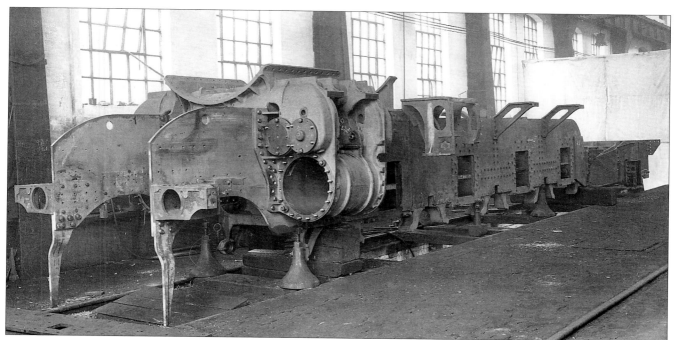

FIG. 201

DON 34/21

The main frames of No. 2001 assembled, to which smoke box saddle, cylinders and running plate support brackets have been fitted, along with the front guard irons.

FIG. 202

DON 34/37

The boiler lagged with Alfol and with its smoke box now fixed to the frames. The front buffer beam has been fitted and the running plate is well under way. Photographed in March 1934 at the Plant.

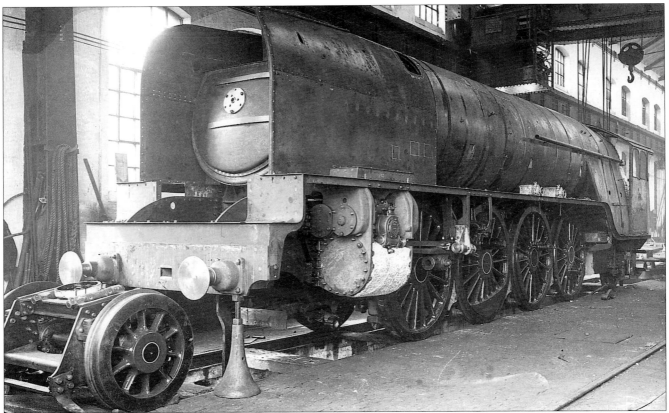

FIG. 203   DON 34/45

Now beginning to take shape with her coupled wheels (already painted and lined out) in situ. The double swing link pony truck is ready to slip into position when the engine is lifted. Front buffers have been added and the shaft for controlling the valve gear is being fitted to the side of the boiler. Photographed in March/April 1934.

FIG. 204   DON 34/92

P2/1 No. 2001. Close-up of the Lentz rotary cam poppet valve gear. The horizontal shaft running along the boiler side was connected via a bevel gearbox to the valve gear by which means the cut-off could be varied or the engine reversed. Photographed on Thursday 19 July 1934.

FIG. 205

DON 34/51

P2/1 No. 2001 *Cock o' the North*, Works No. 1789, built in May 1934 and allocated to Doncaster shed from where she attended exhibitions and took part in many trials, both with and without the dynamometer car, before being reallocated at the end of July to Haymarket where much of her working life would be spent. No. 2001 proved to be very heavy on coal despite having a Kylchap double blast pipe and chimney, and much time and effort was put into trying to cure this voracious appetite, but with very little success. During the mid-sixties the author spent many happy hours in the company of James Cunningham who was the Chief Locomotive Inspector for the Scottish Region. During our many trips out together, much tea drinking and discussion on Gresley engines took place whilst we were waiting for our return workings. When we got round to the P2s, he told me that as a young fireman he had many turns firing 2001 and that he would come off duty soaked to the skin in perspiration and thinking each turn was the hardest work he had done in his life. He finished up by saying in his delightful accent: 'Aye-aye the lassie had a bonny appetite.' In September 1944 Edward Thompson had her back in the Plant to be rebuilt into a Class A2/2 Pacific. This photograph was taken on Wednesday 11 July 1934. She was withdrawn as BR No. 60501 in February 1960.

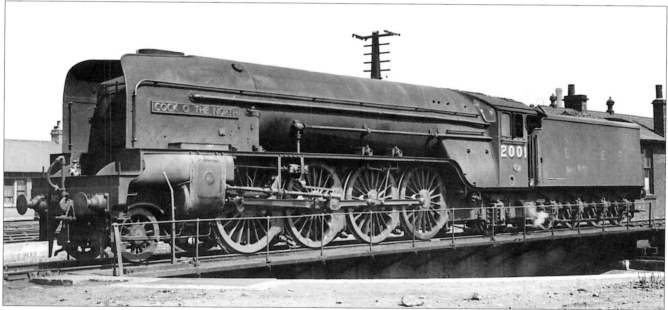

FIG. 206

L. HANSON

No. 2001 on the Haymarket turntable on Sunday 1 August 1937. At this time she was working between Waverley and Dundee. The late T. C. B. Miller told the author that whilst he was shed master at Haymarket in the early days of the war there was a strict embargo on the P2s working trains south of Edinburgh under any circumstances. One night he had a very heavy troop train to work south and, try as he might, he could not find motive power that would have any chance of coping. He did the only thing possible, he put 2001 on with the crew briefed that the moment they had unhooked, turned and taken water they were to return light engine in the hope that she would not be spotted during the blackout. 'After some ten days when nothing had been said I realised that I had got away with it, although at the time it was pretty nerve-racking,' he said with a smile.

FIG. 207

DON 34/62

The front view of 2001 was certainly impressive, the smoke deflectors curving in at the top towards the double chimney with the Crosby tri-tone whistle mounted in front. Little wonder she caused something of a stir when she took to the road. Photographed on Saturday 12 May 1934.

FIG. 208

DON 34/72

The cab of No. 2001 photographed on Monday 28 May 1934. Having Lentz valve gear, she was the only one of her class to have a vertical wheel for operating the reverser.

FIG. 209   DON 34/142

A poor quality photograph which is included for its historical value. No. 2001 is ready to set out for the French locomotive testing station at Vitry-sur-Seine near Paris on Friday 4 December 1934. Hooked on behind her are three 40-ton high capacity coal wagons (lettered 'London and North Eastern Railway, best Yorkshire coal, Yorkshire Main Colliery') carrying the coal she will need for her trials programme, a van containing spare parts and all the necessary tools and equipment that might be needed, with the rear being brought up with a brake van – all being vacuum fitted. She travelled under her own steam, going via Harwich and Calais.

FIG. 210   DON 34/122

P2/1 No. 2002 *Earl Marischal*, Works No. 1796, built in October 1934 and allocated to Doncaster shed whilst undergoing the running-in period. In the following July she was sent north to Haymarket, only to be reallocated to Dundee after just a few weeks. She visibly differed from 2001 in being fitted with Walschaerts valve gear, and is seen here posing for an official photograph on Friday 10 October 1934. In June 1944 Thompson rebuilt No. 2002 into a Pacific of Class A2/2. She was withdrawn as BR No. 60502 in July 1961.

FIG. 211

P2/2 No. 2002 photographed on Thursday 8 October 1936 after emerging from the Plant with her A4-style Bugatti nose. Because of the design of her cylinders it was not possible to enclose the steam pipes from the smoke box to the cylinders. As the boiler was not placed within a streamlined shell, this prevented fitting the side skirts.

FIG. 212   DON 36/76

P2/2 No. 2003 *Lord President*, Works No. 1836, built in June 1936. She was the first of the class of six to be built in streamlined form. The Bugatti nose must have made them very impressive engines. What would you give to be taken back in time to see her, or one of her sisters, roaring through the Scottish country-side, chime whistle blowing, with a train of immaculate teak coaches with white roofs? She went into the Plant in December 1944 to undergo rebuilding into a Class A2/2 Pacific and was withdrawn as BR No. 60503 in November 1959.

FIG. 213   DON 33/66

During the late twenties the Operating Department felt the need for a main line tank engine. The result was the Gresley three-cylinder 2-6-2, designated Class V1. These photographs (above and below) show the frames of possibly No. 2928, Works No. 1799, under construction in August 1933. This assumption is made as that number was in pencil on the back of the official company photograph, as it was on the illustration below which shows the engine at a later stage with the cylinders fitted.

FIG. 214   DON 33/62

FIG. 215   DON 33/57

V1 Class boiler in hydraulic riveter. Photographed in August 1933.

FIG. 216   DON 38/131

V1 No. 451, Works No. 1885, built in October 1938 and fitted with the usual pull/push twin regulator handles, but without water gauge glass protectors. Photographed when new. She was withdrawn as BR No. 67669 in September 1961.

FIG. 217   DON 33/65

V1 Class wheels in balancing machine. Photographed in August 1933.

FIG. 218   L. HANSON

V1 No. 2900, Works No. 1745, built in September 1930 and allocated to Eastfield where this photograph was taken nearly eight years later on Sunday 31 July 1938. She was the first engine of her class, a further 81 being built, the last appearing in February 1939. In March 1956 she was rebuilt to Class V3 which involved the fitting of a 200psi boiler in place of the 180psi boiler fitted when originally built. She was withdrawn as BR No. 67600 in December 1962.

FIG. 219   L. HANSON

V1 No. 2916, Works No. 1761, built in July 1931 and allocated to Haymarket. She is seen passing Princes Street Gardens, Edinburgh on Thursday 4 August 1938. She was rebuilt to Class V3 in May 1960 and was withdrawn as BR No. 67616 in December 1962.

FIG. 220

L. HANSON

V1 No. 2919, Works No. 1764, built in August 1931 and allocated to Eastfield. She was rebuilt to Class V3 in February 1957. In the event 63 of the 82 V1s were to receive the 200 psi boilers by 1961 thus becoming Class V3. This photograph was taken when she was on shed at Eastfield on Tuesday 3 August 1937. She was withdrawn as BR No. 67619 in December 1962.

FIG. 221

L. HANSON

V1 No. 2920, Works No. 1765, built in October 1931 and allocated to Haymarket. Photographed on shed at Eastfield on Sunday 31 July 1938. With the blower on, she is raising steam for her next turn of duty, her bunker being well coaled up. In July 1953 she was rebuilt to Class V3 and was withdrawn as BR No. 67620 in November 1964.

FIG. 222   L. HANSON

V1 No. 2929, Works No. 1801, built in February 1935 and allocated to St Margaret's. Photographed standing out of steam at her home shed on Sunday 1 August 1937. She was never rebuilt, staying Class V1 until she was withdrawn as BR No. 67629 in May 1962.

FIG. 223   L. HANSON

V1 No. 2930, Works No. 1802, built in March 1935 and allocated to St Margaret's. Photographed passing Princes Street Gardens on her way into Edinburgh Waverley with a stopping train on Thursday 4 August 1938. She was never rebuilt, staying Class V1 until she was withdrawn as BR No. 67630 in December 1962.

FIG. 224

DON 36/70

V1 No. 465, Works No. 1835, built in May 1936 and allocated to Blaydon. Photographed just out of the paint shop on Thursday 14 May 1936. She has the new hopper type coal bunker first fitted to her class in November 1935. This arrangement improved the vision through the rear spectacles by a narrowing of the sides. By increasing the height by 10 in. an additional 10 cwt of coal was carried, giving her a capacity of $4\frac{1}{2}$ tons. She remained Class V1, never being rebuilt, and was withdrawn as BR No. 67659 in February 1962.

FIG. 225

DON 38/130

V1 No. 451, Works No. 1885, built in October 1938 and allocated to Cambridge. She was fitted with both vacuum and Westinghouse brakes, a necessity for working on the Great Eastern section. Photographed just out of the paint shop in October 1938, the Westinghouse pump can be seen on the right side front running plate. She was rebuilt to Class V3 in January 1943 and withdrawn as BR No. 67669 in September 1961.

FIG. 226   DON 39/114

V3 No. 390, Works No. 1902, built in September 1939 and allocated to Gateshead. This is her first-of-class photograph taken upon her emergence from the paint shop. She was the first of ten engines to be built as Class V3, all others being rebuilt from Class V1. With the higher boiler pressure previously mentioned and subsequent increase in weight, the tractive effort was increased by nearly 2,500 lb. She was withdrawn as BR No. 67682 in September 1963.

FIG. 227   DON 36/78

V2 No. 637 *Green Arrow*, Works No. 1837, built in June 1936 and allocated to King's Cross. This photograph, taken on Monday 1 June 1936, shows her in her original finish with the nameplates located on the running plates and works plate on the side of the smoke box. She remained in this condition for two days, during which time only three official photographs were taken of her. The LNER negative register has these three crossed through and marked 'not to be used'. As there were no splashers to which the nameplates could be fitted, this layout did not meet with approval and they were moved – the nameplates to the sides of the smoke box and the works plates to the cab sides. At the same time she was renumbered 4771. She was withdrawn as BR No. 60800 in August 1962 and placed in the national collection.

FIG. 228   DON 36/82

Green Arrow with her new number 4771 and straight nameplates affixed to the sides of the smoke box. The same year the class first appeared the four major railway companies had some months previously introduced the Green Arrow Express Goods Service which, for a small supplementary charge, ensured next-day delivery. It was, therefore, an inspired choice to name the new engine *Green Arrow*, thus ensuring not only publicity for the new engine but further advertising the new service which was aimed at the competition from road traffic which at the time was making serious inroads into railway freight business. Some years later this was to be the cause of the railway companies' 'Save Our Railways' square deal campaign. Working from Top Shed she regularly worked the 3.40 p.m. Scotch goods from King's Cross, handing the train over to another engine at Peterborough which would take it forward. After coaling and watering, she would be on a return working to the Cross. I vividly remember this train. It always captured my attention and gets a mention in my Introduction to this book for the smart way in which the vans at Sandy were picked up. The class soon established itself and was equally at home whether it be on fast goods or express passenger trains, and was probably the most useful class the company was ever blessed with. Photographed on Wednesday 3 June 1936.

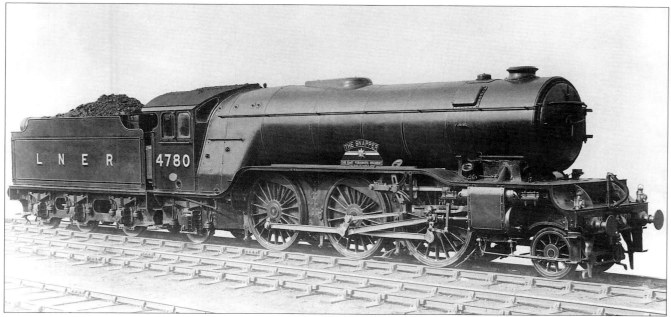

FIG. 229   DON 38/108

V2 No. 4780 *The Snapper, The East Yorkshire Regiment, The Duke of York's Own*, built at Darlington in August 1937 and allocated to York. She had the distinction of being given the longest name of any engine within the company. A total of 184 engines of this class were built, seven receiving names whilst in the service of the LNER and one during BR ownership. Despite the original disapproval, they were all, except for *Green Arrow*, fitted to the running plates, probably because of the awkwardness of the names chosen. Photographed at Darlington when new. She was withdrawn as BR No. 60809 in July 1964.

FIG. 230   DON 39/85

V2 No. 4796, built at Darlington in January 1938 and allocated to Doncaster shed. Photographed on Monday 10 July 1939 after she had undergone a general repair during which Weaver auto brake adjusters had been fitted. She was withdrawn as BR No. 60825 in April 1964.

FIG. 231   L. HANSON

V2 No. 4800, built at Darlington in April 1938 and allocated to Dundee. Photographed on Thursday 4 August 1938, she is seen on the turntable at Haymarket. In October 1938 she was re-allocated to New England, staying in the southern division until she was withdrawn as BR No. 60829 in May 1962.

FIG. 232
AUTHOR'S COLLECTION
Fettling a V2 monobloc cylinder casting.

FIG. 233
AUTHOR'S COLLECTION
Boring a V2 monobloc cylinder casting.

FIG. 234   DON 38/175

V2 No. 4806 *The Green Howard, Alexandra, Princess of Wales's Own Yorkshire Regiment*, built at Darlington in September 1938 and allocated to York. Five of these engines, Nos. 4804-4808, were fitted with multi-valve regulators, the operating linkage being carried externally along the left-hand side of the boiler. These were all removed during the period between 1942 and 1944, thereafter receiving the normal Gresley snifting valve. This engine was fitted with a tender with stepped outside coping plates, a second-hand acquisition from a Class D49. Photographed when new. She was withdrawn as BR No. 60835 in October 1965.

FIG. 235   DON 39/67

V2 No. 4843 *King's Own Yorkshire Light Infantry*, Works No. 1898, built in April 1939 and allocated to Doncaster shed where she spent her working life, except for a sojourn at Grantham for two months in 1961. The Doncaster Plant practice of painting all cylinders black with red lining can be compared with the Darlington practice of painting them green (compare with Figure 234 above – the difference can be seen despite the lack of colour.) Photographed in May 1939. She was withdrawn as BR No. 60872 in September 1963.

130

FIG. 236

V4 No. 3401 *Bantam Cock*, Works No. 1919, was built in February 1941 and allocated to Doncaster shed for two months during the running-in period. This photograph was taken upon emergence from the paint shop in February 1941. The idea behind this design was to produce an engine with a greater route availability, being over 22 tons lighter than the V2 class. After spending twelve months undergoing various trials in the southern division, she was sent to Scotland and remained there until being withdrawn as BR No. 61700 in March 1957.

FIG. 237

V4 No. 3402, Works No. 1920, built in March 1941 and, like her sister, was allocated to Doncaster shed where she spent six months before being sent to Scotland where she was to remain until withdrawn as BR No. 61701 in November 1957. Although never officially named, she was known to the men as *Bantam Hen*. There were a number of differences between the two engines, the most visual being the two different types of dome covers used. This photograph, taken on Thursday 20 March 1941, shows her with a wartime anti-glare cover fitted between the engine and tender.

FIG. 238   DON 40/128

Mid-December 1940, and No. 3401 is taking shape. The boiler and smoke box have been added, the running plate framing and lagging retaining hoops have all been fitted and by 25 February 1941 she will go into traffic.

FIG. 239   AUTHOR'S COLLECTION

W1 No. 10000, built at Yarrow and Darlington in June 1930 and allocated to Gateshead. Built under great secrecy she became known as the 'Hush-Hush' engine to the men in the Plant, a name that was to stay with her. She was unconventional in that she was fitted with a Yarrow marine-type high pressure boiler supplying steam at 450psi to her four compound cylinders, the outside cylinders being low pressure whilst the inside two were high pressure. She was the first 4-6-4 tender engine to be built in this country. Whilst the drawings specified a 4-6-4, it was always contended that she was really a 4-6-2-2. There was insufficient room to fit a rear bogie, so the rear of the engine was carried on two axles, the first having Cartazzi axle boxes whilst the second axle was in the form of a Bisel truck. In November 1937 she was rebuilt with an orthodox boiler and streamlined in a similar manner to the A4s.

FIG. 240

AUTHOR'S COLLECTION

No. 10000 posing for her official photograph in 1930. Finished in dark grey with stainless steel boiler bands, white lettering and numerals shaded in black, her appearance caused quite a sensation at the time.

FIG. 241

AUTHOR'S COLLECTION

In August 1930 she returned to the Darlington works for various repairs and modifications to be carried out, not being returned to traffic until the following January. During this time she was made available for participation in the centenary celebrations of the opening of the Liverpool and Manchester Railway in September. This photograph, taken early in October 1930, shows her on the turntable at Agecroft prior to returning to Darlington works.

DON 37/169

FIG. 242

W1 No. 10000 entered the Plant for rebuilding into a three-cylinder simple engine in October 1936. When this photograph was taken in October 1937 she had just emerged from the paint shop for her official picture. In her rebuilt form she resembled an A4, finished in Garter Blue with Coronation Red wheels. Unlike her A4 sisters, she had a slight bulge in her streamlined casing to accommodate her cylinders. She entered traffic on 6 November 1937 and was allocated to King's Cross. A novel feature that was retained from the original engine was the illumination of the motion by lights concealed under the side valances of the streamlined casing. She was withdrawn as BR No. 60700 in June 1959.

'50 YEARS BACK'

With the introduction of the new 1938 summer service, the company provided new stock for their world-famous 'Flying Scotsman' train, the 10 a.m., as it was originally known, which ran non-stop in both directions with a similar departure time from Edinburgh. Showing their usual flair for publicity, the company decided it would re-run the 10 a.m. of 50 years back.

Stirling Single No. 1 was disturbed from her slumbers in the old York Railway Museum and sent off to the Plant to be made steamworthy and put into good mechanical condition. The system was then combed for old six-wheeled coaches. Eventually seven were assembled and they were put through the Plant's carriage shop for both interior and exterior renovation. This train, along with the new Flying Scotsman train – headed by A4 No. 4498 *Sir Nigel*

Gresley – ran for invited company guests on Thursday 30 June 1938.

Such was the clamour from the public to ride the old train that a special excursion to Cambridge was run on Wednesday 24 August. The RCTS (Railway Correspondence and Travel Society) finding that many of their members were unable to take part during the week, chartered the train and ran a special to Peterborough and back on Sunday 11 September 1938. Leslie Hanson was fortunate to have taken part and his camera duly recorded this great day out.

The crew of the train on this historic trip comprised Guard Smitten (in charge of the train), Driver A. Hoskins and Fireman C. E. Thomas; with Locomotive Inspector Bramwell also travelling on the footplate – all King's Cross men.

FIG. 243   L. HANSON

After taking water at Huntingdon on the down journey, Driver Hoskins of King's Cross Top Shed, waits for the right of way. The Stirling horizontal pull/push regulator handle is clearly visible. Note also the coal in the tender. This did not come from Top Shed's coaling plant. No chances were being taken with bad steaming, and lumps of the right size were hand-picked, so the late Cyril Palmer told me. At that time he was involved with the maintenance of No. 1 at Top Shed whilst she was running these special trains. When he died in 1965, C. G. Palmer was Line Manager (Great Northern Section).

FIG. 244   L. HANSON

After arrival at Peterborough, waiting for the train to be pulled out, whereupon No. 1 with tail light on the front will follow. Note the RCTS headboard on the top lamp bracket. This was the first occasion of a railway society hiring a train and running an excursion for the sole use of its members.

FIG. 245   L. HANSON

The Flying Scotsman of 1888 was usually made up of seven six-wheel coaches. Not having corridors or lavatory accommodation was very limiting, and of course no dining car was provided. A special stop of 20 minutes was made at York to enable passengers to partake of refreshment at the station buffet. If the train was full there was a potential 80 first-class and 90 third-class passengers on board. There had to be some pretty smart counter service to supply even a quarter of this number, especially if hot drinks were required. One can almost feel the relief of the staff when the first blast of the guard's whistle caused a rapid exit back to the train. It would be interesting to know how many of the first class passengers indulged in this skirmish and how many brought their own hampers. Here at Peterborough we can see the result of Doncaster's efforts in preservation. Sadly, no one had the sense, or more likely the space, to store them and they were duly broken up.

FIG. 246

L. HANSON

At Peterborough, prior to commencing the return journey to King's Cross. The 8 ft. diameter driving wheel shows up well in this photograph, as does the spartan shelter afforded by the cab. For many enthusiasts this was the first time that they had seen a single-wheeler in steam. The excitement was all the greater for the lucky few who were allowed a brief visit to the footplate.

FIG. 247

L. HANSON

After arriving at King's Cross. The fireman has just placed the red tail lamp on the front buffer beam and awaits the removal of the coaches whereupon she will back down to the platform starting signal where she will wait for her path to Top Shed.

FIG. 248   DON 45/42

Edward Thompson, Colonel Bingham (US Army) and Arthur Peppercorn after inspecting General Eisenhower's special armour-plated coach on Monday 12 March 1945. This vehicle, No. 1591, was originally built in 1936 to Diagram 157 as a First-class sleeping car with ten single compartments.

FIG. 249   DON 45/45

Interior of General Eisenhower's saloon photographed from the doorway leading to his sleeping quarters. Note the air-conditioning unit fitted on the end wall.

FIG. 250

DON 45/23

The adjoining coach to General Eisenhower's saloon, No. 1592, built in 1936 to the same diagram as No. 1591. When in use they travelled under the code name 'Bayonet'. This photograph is of the interior of the saloon taken from the corridor leading to the sleeping berths.

FIG. 251

DON 45/22

The opposite end view of coach 1592 photographed from the entrance. Both coaches were finished outside in green to match the stock of the Southern Railway, the company over whose tracks the train would mainly be operated.

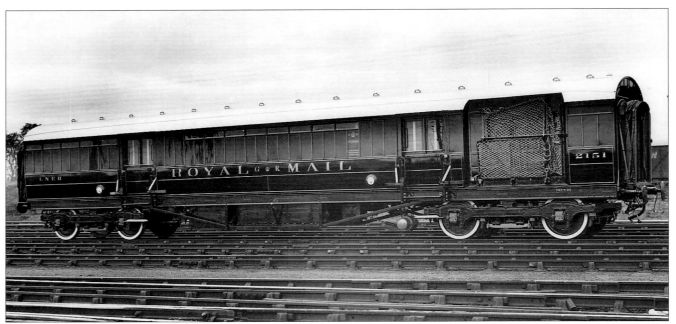

FIG. 252   AUTHOR'S COLLECTION

Post Office sorting van No. 2151 built at York in April 1933 to Diagram 0165 at a cost of £2,500. It was 60 ft. 2in. long and weighed 33 tons. A single lavatory was provided. It was renumbered on Saturday 16 March 1946 becoming No. 70300. Photographed at York when new in April 1933.

FIG. 253   AUTHOR'S COLLECTION

Close-up view of the collecting net and traductor arms of Post Office sorting van No. 2154 which was built in 1933 to the same diagram as No. 2151 pictured above. It was renumbered 70303 on Saturday 30 March 1946. Note the mail box located above the letter 'L' (of MAIL). Letters posted here had to bear an additional ½d stamp.

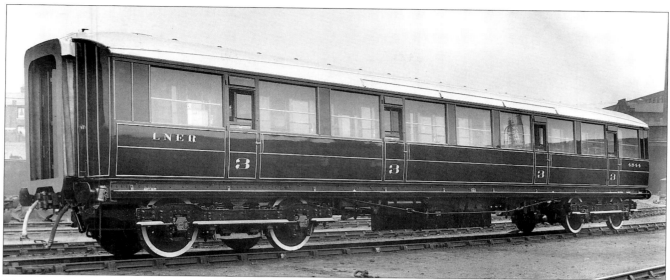

FIG. 254   AUTHOR'S COLLECTION

Third-class coach No. 4844 built at Dukinfield in 1927 to Diagram 23 at a cost of £2,720. It was 61 ft. 6 in. long and weighed 35 tons. Eight compartments giving seating for 64 passengers. Two lavatories were provided. It was renumbered on Saturday 10 February 1945, becoming No. 12056.

FIG. 255   DON 28/20

Semi-open First-class coach No. 4234 built in January 1928 to Diagram 5 at a cost of £3,655. It was 61 ft. 6 in. long and weighed 33 tons. Five compartments provided seating for 42 passengers. Lavatory accommodation was not provided. It was renumbered on Saturday 11 November 1944, becoming No. 11041. This photograph was taken on Tuesday 31 January 1928.

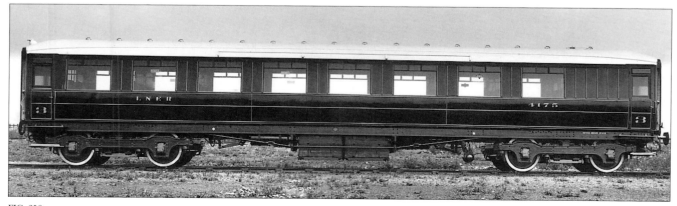

FIG. 256   DON 31/102

Open Third-class coach No. 4175 built in July 1931 to Diagram 150 at a cost of £2,780. Two compartments seated 64 passengers with single lavatory accommodation. It was renumbered on Saturday 3 November 1945, becoming No. 12927. This photograph was taken on Monday 6 July 1931.

FIG. 257   DON 34/93

First-class coach No. 6461 built in July 1934 to Diagram 140 at a cost of £2,623. It was 52 ft. 6 in. long and weighed 32 tons. There were six compartments seating 36 passengers. Two lavatories were provided. This photograph was taken on Saturday 21 July 1934.

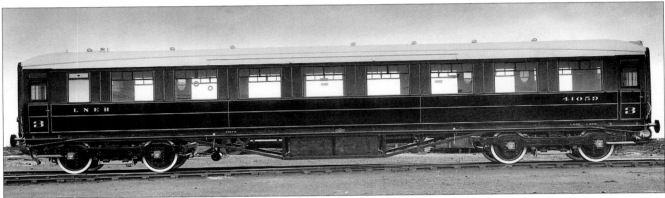

FIG. 258   DON 36/223

Open Third-class coach No. 41059 built by Cravens in November 1936 to Diagram 27c at a cost of £2,800. It was 61 ft. 6 in. long and weighed 33 tons. There were two compartments seating 48 passengers. One lavatory was provided. It was renumbered on Monday 27 October 1945, becoming No. 12217. This photograph was taken on Monday 2 November 1936.

FIG. 259   DON 44/204

Composite First/Third coach No. 51896 built at York in April 1938 to Diagram 137 at a cost of £2,653, photographed when new. It was 61 ft. 6 in. long and weighed 33 tons. Two First-class compartments seated 12 passengers with a First-class coupé providing a further three seats. Five Third-class compartments accommodated 30 passengers. Two lavatories were provided. It was renumbered on Saturday 20 January 1945, becoming No. 18320.

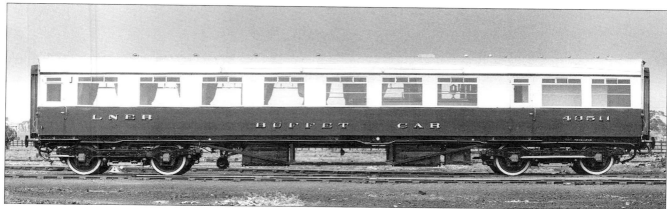

FIG. 260

DON 33/52

Third-class tourist stock buffet car No. 43511, built at York in 1933 to diagram 0168 at a cost of £2,644 (renumbered 9145 on Saturday 2 June 1945). It was 61 ft. 6 in. long and weighed 33 tons. A gas kitchen was provided and a single compartment seated 24 diners. With the country slowly recovering from the slump, the company could see a growing demand for cheap day excursions. Such traffic had previously been handled by using obsolete coaches, but something much better was needed to catch the new market, and in 1933 the Board sanctioned the building of five 12-coach trains, each to consist of four twin-articulated open Thirds, two buffet cars and two open brake Thirds. Whilst the normal teak framing was used for the bodies, panelling (both inside and outside) was of ¼ in. marine three-ply in place of teak to keep the cost down. Inside panelling was covered in Rexine, and with the outsides painted cream above the waist and engine green below, and white-painted roofs, they had a most attractive appearance.

FIG. 261

DON 30/3

First-class restaurant car No. 31922 built in January 1930 to Diagram 11 at a cost of £3,656. Two compartments seated 30 diners and an electric kitchen was fitted. Single lavatory accommodation was provided. It was renumbered on Saturday 17 September 1949, becoming No. 9023. This photograph was taken on Monday 13 January 1930.

FIG. 262

AUTHOR'S COLLECTION

Third-class sleeping car No. 1336 built at York in 1931 to Diagram 148 at a cost of £3,094. It was 66 ft. 6in. long and weighed 38 tons. Eight compartments provided sleeping accommodation for 32 passengers. Two lavatories were fitted but no compartment was provided for an attendant.

FIG. 263   DON 31/7

First-class brake No. 22611 built in December 1930 to Diagram 142 at a cost of £2,272. It was 61 ft. 6 in. long and weighed 32 tons. Two compartments seated 12 passengers with single lavatory accommodation. Rescue appliances were fitted. It was renumbered on Saturday 12 May 1945, becoming No. 11062. This photograph was taken on Monday 12 January 1931.

FIG. 264   DON 32/41

Third-class brake No. 62648 built in February 1932 to Diagram 146 at a cost of £2,007. It was 52 ft. 6 in. long and weighed 30 tons. Three compartments seated 24 passengers with single lavatory accommodation. Rescue appliances were fitted. This photograph was taken on Friday 11 March 1932.

FIG. 265   DON 32/92

Composite First/Third brake No. 495 built at Dukinfield in August 1932 to Diagram 134 at a cost of £2,639. It was 61 ft. 6 in. long and weighed 34 tons. There were two First-class compartments seating 12 passengers with four Third-class compartments accommodating 24 passengers. Two lavatories were provided. It was renumbered on Saturday 4 August 1945, becoming No. 10049. This photograph was taken on Friday 19 August 1932.

GOODS WAGONS

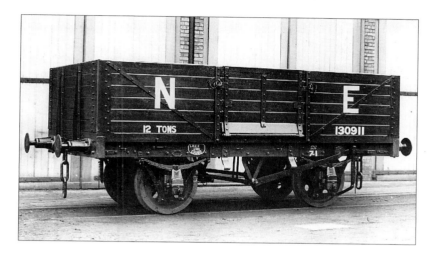

FIG. 266 DON 24/7

12-ton, six-plank open goods wagon No. 130911, with single-flap door on each side. Fitted with a brake lever on both sides. Photographed on Tuesday 29 January 1924.

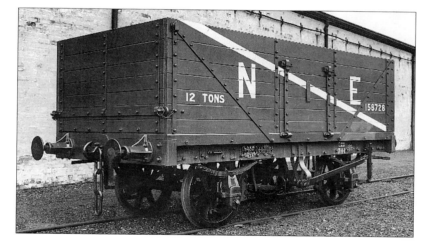

FIG. 267 DON 30/2

12-ton standard end-door mineral wagon No. 158728 with a single-flap door on each side. Fitted with a brake lever on both sides. Built by the Birmingham Carriage & Wagon Company Limited in 1929. Photographed at the Plant on Thursday 9 January 1930.

FIG. 268 DON 31/57

Six-ton, three-plank open wagon No. 416850 with a single-flap door on each side, radiused ends and a longitudinal tarpaulin pole. Fitted with vacuum brakes, screw couplings and a brake lever on both sides. Originally built as a fish wagon and converted, which is probably the reason for the photograph being taken on Friday 10 April 1931.

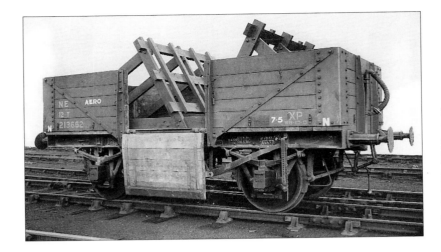

FIG. 269   DON 39/133

12-ton, five-plank open goods wagon No. 213662 with a single-flap door on each side. It has been adapted for carrying aeroplane propellors by the installation of special cradles into which they were secured. Fitted with vacuum brakes and screw couplings with with a brake lever on both sides. Photographed on Saturday 18 November 1939.

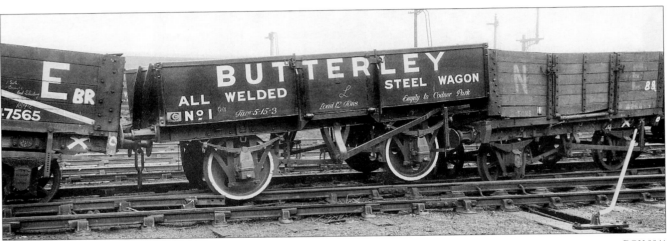

FIG. 270   DON 36/4

ABOVE AND BELOW

Butterley 12-ton all steel, all welded open wagon No. 1 fitted with a brake lever on both sides. These photographs show the durability of the welded steel wagon when tested in a deliberate heavy shunt staged in January 1936.

FIG. 271   DON 36/6

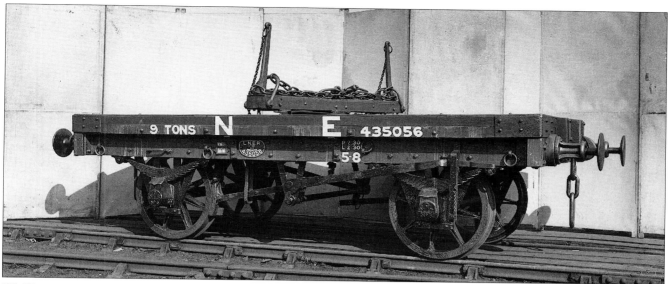

FIG. 272

DON 30/87

9-ton short timber wagon No. 435056 fitted with a steel bolster with a brake lever on both sides and split-spoked wheels. Photographed on Friday 14 March 1930.

FIG. 273   DON 41/36

12-ton container flat wagon No. 175798, built in 1931, loaded with insulated meat container No. FM 191. Fitted with vacuum brakes and screw couplings with a brake lever on both sides. Photographed to show the new container on Wednesday 7 May 1941.

FIG. 274   DON 32/90

12-ton container flat wagon No. 170627, Loaded with container No. BLG 519. Fitted with vacuum brakes, screw couplings, and a brake lever on both sides. Photographed on Saturday 13 August 1932.

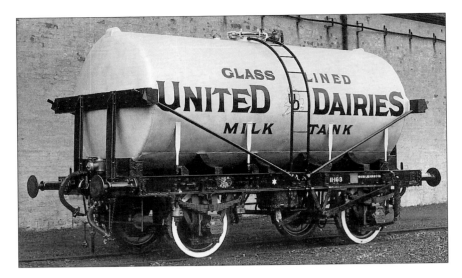

FIG. 275   DON 30/86

United Dairies glass-lined milk tank wagon No. 4306. Fitted with vacuum brakes, screw couplings and a brake lever on both sides. Lamp brackets were provided at each end to carry a tail lamp when attached to the rear of a passenger or milk train. Photographed on Friday 14 March 1930.

FIG. 276   AUTHOR'S COLLECTION

Six-wheel flat truck No. 203878 with removable I.C.I. twin tanks. Fitted with vacuum brakes, screw couplings and a brake lever on both sides. Inscribed 'EMPTY TO I.C.I. (F.&S.P. Ltd) SIDINGS HAVERTON HILL'. Built at Darlington and photographed when new in November 1937.

FIG. 277   DON 27/27

12-ton covered goods van No. 151217 with a single door on each side. Fitted with a brake lever on both sides. Photographed when new on Thursday 10 March 1927.

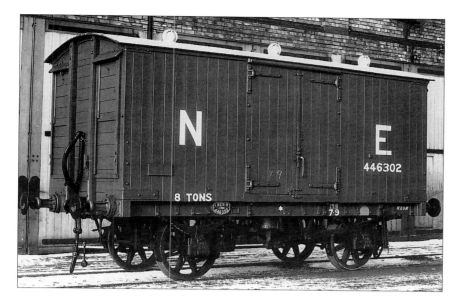

FIG. 278   DON 24/1

8-ton express covered ventilated goods van No. 446302 with double doors on each side. Fitted with vacuum brakes, screw couplings and a brake lever on both sides. This vehicle was converted from a banana van which was probably the reason for the taking of the photograph on Wednesday 9 January 1924.

FIG. 279   DON 25/61

3-ton, long wheel-base covered goods van No. 408914, with two double doors on each side. Fitted with vacuum brakes and screw couplings. Inscribed on the side was 'To work between LUTON & KING'S CROSS WITH HAT TRAFFIC.' Photographed on Thursday 16 July 1925.

FIG. 280   DON 26/10

4-ton covered carriage truck No. 303 with double doors at each end for vehicular access, and double doors on each side. Whilst it is officially listed as a carriage truck, by the time this photograph was taken it would, no doubt, also have been used for motor car traffic. Fitted with both vacuum and Westinghouse brakes, screw couplings and a brake lever on both sides. Photographed when new at the Plant on Thursday 4 March 1926.

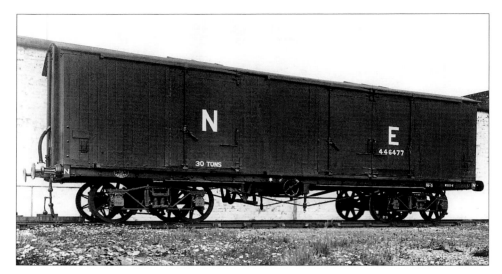

FIG. 281   DON 27/133

30-ton express covered goods van No. 446477 with a double and single door on each side. Fitted with vacuum brakes, screw couplings and a wheel brake on both sides. Photographed on Thursday 25 August 1927.

FIG. 282   DON 41/25

10-ton ventilated meat and perishable van No. 15841 built at Darlington in 1924. With a single door on each side and fitted with vacuum brakes, screw couplings and a brake lever on both sides. Lamp brackets were provided at each end to carry a tail lamp when attached to the rear of a passenger train. Photographed at the Plant after being overhauled and repainted on Tuesday 8 April 1941.

FIG. 283   DON 31/188

10-ton ventilated perishable van No. 161505 with a single door on each side. Fitted with vacuum brakes, screw couplings and a brake lever on both sides. Lamp brackets were provided at each end to carry a tail lamp when attached to the rear of passenger trains. Photographed in November 1931.

FIG. 284   DON 45/82

Tunnel inspection van No. NE 950230 allocated to the Nottingham district for working out of Colwick. Fitted with a brake lever on both sides and screw couplings to avoid jolting the inspectors off the roof when being propelled through tunnels. How many model railways feature such a vehicle? There is scope here for the enthusiastic modeller. Photographed on Monday 14 May 1945.

FIG. 285   DON 30/181

20-ton goods brake van No. 162013 with steel viewing projections. Fitted with sanding gear, three-link couplings and split-spoked wheels. Photographed on Friday 10 October 1930.

FIG. 286   DON 67/484

20-ton goods brake van No. 235109 fitted with vacuum brakes and screw couplings. The company laid great store by their fast goods trains, many of which averaged 50 mph over long distances. Guards regularly complained about the rough riding of the standard 12 ft. wheel base van, and in 1929 the first 16 ft. wheel base van was built at Darlington to deal with the problem. The late Norman Newsome, who at that time was working with Frank Day, the technical assistant for carriage and wagon development at King's Cross, told how it fell to him to report on the riding of the new vehicle at speed. It was attached to the rear of an express which regularly reached 75 mph between London and Hitchin. He recalled how he felt a certain amount of trepidation when his colleagues all turned out to wave him off. Returning to the Cross later that day behind another fast train, he reported that it rode extremely well and it became the company's standard express goods brake van. This photograph is a copy of an original Darlington Drawing Office print copied at the Plant on Friday 26 September 1967.

HORSE DRAWN ROAD VEHICLES

FIG. 287   DON 24/47

2-ton road van Fleet No. N1354, allocated to Kensington depot, photographed when new on Wednesday 19 November 1924.

FIG. 288   DON 25/3

15-cwt parcels van Fleet No. N1754, photographed when new on Tuesday 13 January 1925.

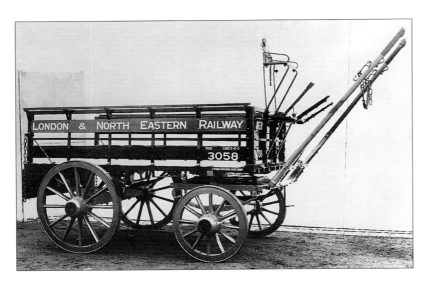

FIG. 289   DON 30/151

Single horse 2½-ton dray Fleet No. 3058, photographed when new on Friday 20 June 1930.

MOTOR ROAD VEHICLES

FIG. 290   DON 25/75
Ford Model T 1-ton motor lorry Fleet No. N66 photographed when new on Thursday 1 October 1925.

FIG. 291   DON 28/116
Albion 2-ton motor lorry Fleet No. 436 photographed when new on Wednesday 27 September 1928.

FIG. 292   DON 29/106
ADC (Associated Daimler Co.) 2-ton motor lorry with high-sided body and loose tilt, Fleet No. 575, photographed when new on Friday 30 August 1929.

FIG. 293   AUTHOR'S COLLECTION

Guy horse box (Registration No. FUL 712) Fleet No. BS 0102, photographed when new on Thursday 22 March 1945.

FIG. 294   DON 45/166

Scammel mechanical horse (Registration No. EGT 866) Fleet No. HD 6044, photographed when new on Tuesday 23 October 1945.

FIG. 295   DON 44/60

3-ton flat trailer for use with Scammel mechanical horse tractor unit, Fleet No. CT2408, photographed when new on Friday 28 March 1944.

WATER SOFTENING AND COALING PLANTS

FIG. 296   DON 35/115

Langley water softening plant photographed not long after completion in August 1935, erected at a cost of £2,730 and capable of treating 100 million gallons of water per year. The old GN tender now lettered 'Service Stock Sludge Carrier Langley' stands in its own siding ready to collect the chalk-like sludge.

FIG. 297   DON 36/271

Essendine water softening plant, photographed shortly after completion on Thursday 31 December 1936. Costing £2,024, it could soften 25 million gallons of water per year. The usual ex-GN tender fitted with buffers and draw hook is in attendance.

FIG. 298   DON 34/96

Offord water softening plant shortly after completion on Friday 29 April 1926, built at a cost of £2,233 to soften 24 million gallons of water per year. Two ex-GN tenders converted into sludge carriers are in attendance.

FIG. 299 DON 35/31

Whitemoor mechanical coaling plant built in 1928 and photographed on Wednesday 6 March 1935. It had a capacity of 500 tons. A steel bodied 20-ton wagon is being hoisted up to the top, prior to its load being tipped into the hopper.

FIG. 300 DON 38/112

Coaling plant at Ardsley Loco, photographed on Friday 19 August 1938.

FIG. 301 DON 26/62

Doncaster Carr shed mechanical coaling plant, photographed on Monday 4 October 1926. A C1 Atlantic poses on one side of the plant, and an ex-GN six-wheel coach mounted on brick piers serves as a mess hut.

STEAM CRANES

FIG. 302   DON 37/15

New England wet ash pit which was built in the early thirties as part of the LNER improvement scheme. The Booth Rodley steam crane is taking the ash and clinker from the pit and loading it into empty wagons on the adjacent road. In the background is the new 500-ton mechanical coaling plant (centre left) and the old 1905 coal stage (centre right). In the distance on the far right are the main sheds. Photographed in March 1937.

FIG. 303   DON 42/104

Sentinel steam crane with grab, possibly giving a demonstration as it is in unfinished condition. Intended for ash disposal at engine sheds it is probably not on railway land as this is a copy print and the rather interesting articulated Sentinel waggon in the background suggests it may have been at the Sentinel works.

FIG. 304   DON 37/19

The Booth Rodley steam crane with grab which was used at New England Loco for emptying the fire dropping pits. Photographed in March 1937.

FIG. 305   AUTHOR'S COLLECTION

7-ton steam crane No. 773082 built by Henry Coles Ltd, and runner No. 773083 (labelled 'Engineer's Department, Central District') based at Portobello.

REFRESHMENT AND OTHER TROLLEYS

FIG. 306   DON 37/27

New type platform refreshment trolley, photographed when new in March 1937.

FIG. 307   DON 39/26

The LNER negative register describes this trolley in the following terms: 'Trailer barrow for coaling New Holland ferry.' It must have been an economical boiler! Photographed on Tuesday 21 March 1939.

RAIL BUILT BUFFER STOPS AND GROUND SHUNT SIGNAL

FIG. 308   AUTHOR

Rail built buffer stops adjacent to New England Loco which survived the LNER era well into British Rail days. Photographed on Saturday 9 April 1955.

FIG. 309   AUTHOR

Another view of the rail built buffer stops to aid the modeller. Note the high mounted red light which is high enough to be seen by the driver of the shunting engine above the height of the wagons which he is propelling into the siding.

FIG. 310   AUTHOR

Ground signal in New England goods yard adjacent to the loco sheds. Photographed on Saturday 9 April 1955.

SELECTED COMPANY MINUTES

of the Joint Locomotive and Traffic Committees

At a JOINT MEETING of the LOCOMOTIVE AND TRAFFIC COMMITTEES held at MARYLEBONE STATION, LONDON, on THURSDAY, 28th JULY 1927.

FILE COPY.

PRESENT:

WILLIAM WHITELAW, ESQ., In the Chair.
H. T. Bailey, Esq.,
Sir Charles C. Barrie, K.B.E.,
The Hon. Rupert E. Beckett,
O. R. H. Bury, Esq.,
The Hon. Eric B. Butler-Henderson,
B. A. Firth, Esq.,
W. B. Gair, Esq.,
Colonel Wm. Johnson Galloway,
A. R. Gray, Esq.,
The Rt. Hon. Viscount Grey of Fallodon, K.G.,
A. K. McCosh, Esq.,
Sir Arthur F. Pease, Bart.,
F. L. Steel, Esq.,
W. K. Whigham, Esq.,
Sir Murrough J. Wilson.,K.B.E., M.P.

L. & N. E. R. SECRETARY'S OFFICE APPROVED BY BOARD 29 JUL 1927

Attended by:

Sir R. L. Wedgwood, C.B., C.M.G.,
Mr. Wickham,
Mr. Gresley,
Mr. Calder,
Mr. Davidson,
Mr. Wilson,
Mr. Oldham,
Mr. Clow,
Mr. Maclure,
Mr. Selway,
Mr. James McLaren, Secretary,
Mr. P. J. Dowsett, Assistant Secretary.

23. Minutes of the last joint Meeting (24th March 1927) were approved and signed.

X.W 4177.

24. LOCOMOTIVE BUILDING PROGRAMME, 1928.

With reference to Minute No. 18; submitted Memorandum by the Chief General Manager reporting that the stock of engines at completion of the Programme originally sanctioned for the year ended 31st March 1927 and extended to cover the period ending 31st December 1927 will be 7,495 (Tender 4,795, Tank 2,687, Electric 13).

It is estimated that it will be necessary to break up 200 engines (Tender 146 and Tank 54) in order to maintain efficiently the locomotive power of the Company, and he recommended that 131

1.

FIG. 311

24
con.

engines of the undermentioned types should be built :

TENDER ENGINES.

4. 6. 2. Passenger	10.	
4. 4. 0. "	8.	
2. 6. 0. Express Goods	20.	
0. 6. 0. Goods	52.	90.

TANK ENGINES.

2. 6. 4. Passenger	12.	
0. 6. 2. "	29.	41.
	Total	131.

In addition it is proposed to recondition
2. 8. 0. Government Engines   30.

He further recommended the provision of 50 Sentinel Cammell Steam Rail Cars at an estimated total cost of £ 190,000 and 4 Super Sentinel Locomotives at a cost of £ 5,600.   It was considered that one half only of the cost of the former should be debited to the Locomotive Programme, the remainder falling to be debited to the Carriage Building Programme to be presented later in the year.

The estimated cost of the full Programme (including the £ 95,000 to be debited to the Carriage Building Programme) is £ 975,720.

RESOLVED

THAT the Programme submitted be approved generally and recommended to the Board for adoption.

Further that it be remitted :

(1) to the Locomotive Committee to decide where the building and re-conditioning of the Locomotives be undertaken at an estimated cost of £ 780,120; and

(2) to the Chairman, Mr. Firth, and the Chief Mechanical Engineer to place orders for 50 Steam Rail Motorcars and 4 Super Sentinel Light Shunting Locomotives at an estimated cost of £ 195,600.

2.

FIG. 312   AUTHOR'S COLLECTION

162

At a JOINT MEETING of the LOCOMOTIVE AND TRAFFIC COMMITTEES held at MARYLEBONE STATION, LONDON, on THURSDAY, 27th OCTOBER 1927.

PRESENT:

WILLIAM WHITELAW, ESQ., In the Chair.
The Rt. Hon. Lord Faringdon, C.H.,
H. T. Bailey, Esq.,
Sir C. C. Barrie, K.B.E.,
The Hon. Rupert E. Beckett,
Sir Hugh Bell, Bart., C.B.,
O. R. H. Bury, Esq.,
The Hon. Eric B. Butler-Henderson,
B. A. Firth, Esq.,
W. B. Gair, Esq.,
Colonel Wm. Johnson Galloway,
A. R. Gray, Esq.,
The Rt. Hon. Viscount Grey of Fallodon, K.G.,
A. K. McCosh, Esq.,
F. L. Steel, Esq.,
Sir Murrough J. Wilson, K.B.E., M.P.

Attended by:

Sir R. L. Wedgwood, C.B., C.M.G.,
Mr. Train,
Mr. Gresley,
Mr. Wilson,
Mr. Oldham,
Mr. Marshall,
Mr. Calder,
Mr. Davidson,
Mr. Edwards,
The Secretary and
Assistant Secretary.

L. & N. E. R.
SECRETARY'S OFFICE
APPROVED BY
BOARD
28 OCT 1927

25. Minutes of last joint Meeting (28th July 1927) were signed.

XW. 3973

26. WAGON BUILDING PROGRAMME, 1928.

Submitted Memorandum, dated October 18th 1927, from the Chief General Manager on the proposed Wagon Building Programme for the year 1928. It is estimated that 9,850 wagons will be broken up during the year 1928 and it is proposed to replace these by the construction of 8,615 wagons, (a reduction of 1,235) at an estimated cost of £ 1,529,280, the new wagons to comprise

1.

FIG. 313

AUTHOR'S COLLECTION

26
con.

the following types, all of which it is proposed to construct in the Company's Shops, as follow :

TYPE.	Number to be Built.		Estimated Cost. £
Goods Wagons, open, unfitted	2,530	12-ton)	367,130.
	120	20-ton)	
" " " fitted.	50	12-ton	8,300.
Goods Wagons, covered, unfitted	1,000	12-ton	180,000.
" " " fitted	1,000	12-ton	210,000.
Fish Wagons, covered	40	10-ton	10,400.
" " open	-		-
Refrigerator Vans	5	8-ton	2,450.
Rail and Timber Trucks	120	40-ton)	102,800.
	200	12-ton)	
Cattle Trucks, unfitted	200	10-ton	35,000.
" " fitted	70	10-ton	14,350.
Special	-		-
Mineral Wagons (end door)	1,500	12-ton	210,000.
All other Mineral Wagons	1,500	20-ton	300,000.
Brake Vans	130	20-ton	61,100.
Locomotive Coal Wagons	150	20-ton	27,750.
	8,615.		£ 1,529,280.

It is also estimated that 90 "common user" coaching vehicles will be broken up in the same period, which it is not proposed to replace.

IT WAS RESOLVED

To RECOMMEND to the Board the building of the wagons proposed in the Chief General Manager's Memorandum covering a period to be decided later.

2.

FIG. 314   AUTHOR'S COLLECTION

164

FILE COPY

At a Meeting of the LOCOMOTIVE COMMITTEE, held at Marylebone Station, London, on Thursday, the 7th day of January, 1932.

L.& N.E.R. CRETARY'S OFFICE PPROVED BY BOARD 8 JAN 1932

PRESENT:

A. K. McCOSH, ESQ., in the Chair.

The Rt. Hon. Lord Faringdon, C.H.,

The Rt. Hon. Viscount Grey of Fallodon, K.G.,

W. B. Gair, Esq.

Attended by:

Sir Ralph Wedgwood,
Mr. Newton,
Mr. Gresley,
Mr. Stamer,
Mr. Richards,
Mr. Groom,
Mr. Dowsett, Assistant Secretary.

1451. The Minutes of Meeting held on 26th November, 1931, were read and confirmed.

1452. Statements for four weeks and aggregate of forty-four weeks to 31st October, 1931, were submitted as under:-

(a) Revenue Expenditure - Maintenance of Rolling Stock.
(b) Revenue Expenditure - Locomotive Running Expenses.
(c) Maintenance & Renewal of Rolling Stock - Statistics.
(d) Engine Failures - Summary.
(e) New Rolling Stock sent into traffic.

XW.757

1453. YORK: SUPPLY OF ELECTRICAL ENERGY.

The Chief Mechanical Engineer reported that under the Electricity Bulk Supply Agreement with the York Corporation, authorised by Minute No.133, the cost of 2,203,050 units during the year 1930 amounted to £11,223, equivalent to 1·22d. per unit.

An effort has been made to obtain lower terms, and the Corporation have offered, subject to a new Agreement for 10 years being entered into from January 1st, 1932, the following revised terms:-

(Continued).

1.

FIG. 315 AUTHOR'S COLLECTION

1453.
Contd.

(1) <u>HIGH TENSION SUPPLY TO LEEMAN ROAD SUB-STATION.</u>

Maximum Demand Charge   -   £4: 10: 0d. per K.V.A.

Unit Charge   -   For the first million units per annum 0·35d. per unit.

For all in excess of one million units 0·3d. per unit.

(2) <u>LOW TENSION SUPPLY TO BAR WALLS.</u>

Maximum Demand Charge   -   £6 per K.W.

Unit Charge   -   0.65d. per unit.

In accordance with these terms the total cost per annum would be reduced to £8,847., equivalent to 0·96d. per unit, thereby representing a saving of £2,376 per annum.

It was recommended that a new Agreement be completed accordingly.

APPROVED.

XW. 6424

1461. SCARBOROUGH, WHITBY AND SALTBURN BRANCH:
STEAM COACHES.

Referring to Minute No.1450(d); submitted Memorandum by the Chief Mechanical Engineer together with quotation by the "Sentinel" Waggon Works Ltd., for three 200 H.P. single type Rail Coaches, 63' 6" long, fitted with bucket type seats, at £5,780 each, or a total of £17,340 for the three coaches, delivery to be effected in six months' time. The original estimate for three coaches at £5,230 each, making a total of £15,690, was based on coaches similar to the two authorised by Minute No.974, whereas the new coaches are slightly longer and the seating accommodation is increased and of a more luxurious type.

It was recommended that the order be placed at the price quoted.

APPROVED.

5.

FIG. 316   AUTHOR'S COLLECTION

166

At a Meeting of the TRAFFIC COMMITTEE, held at Marylebone Station, London, on Thursday, the 17th day of March, 1932.

PRESENT:

THE RT. HON. VISCOUNT GREY OF FALLODON, K.G.; in the Chair.

William Whitelaw, Esq.,

H. T. Bailey, Esq.,

Sir Charles C. Barrie, M.P.,

Sir Charles A. Batho, Bart.,

O. R. H. Bury, Esq.,

The Hon. E. B. Butler-Henderson,

Major W. H. Carver, M.P.,

A. R. Gray, Esq.,

R. W. Matthews, Esq.,

Clarence D. Smith, Esq.,

F. L. Steel, Esq.,

Sir Murrough J. Wilson.

Attended by:

Sir Ralph Wedgwood,
Mr. Teasdale,
Mr. Hornsby,
Mr. Thurston,
Mr. Oldham,
Mr. Barrington-Ward,
Mr. Brickwell,
Mr. Marshall,
Mr. Mauldin,
Mr. Selway,
Mr. Gresley,
Mr. Stamer,
Mr. McLaren, Secretary.

1997.   Minutes of last Meeting (18th February) were read, confirmed and signed.

1998.   The following Returns were submitted:-

(a) Traffic Expenses, 4 weeks ended 30th January, 1932.
(b) Revenue Returns, 4 weeks ended 27th February, 1932.
(c) Running of Passenger Trains.
(d) Running of Freight Trains.
(e) Loaded Wagons Forwarded.
(f) Receipts and Expenditure in respect of Docks, Harbours and Wharves, 4 weeks ended 30th January, 1932.

1.

FIG. 317   AUTHOR'S COLLECTION

167

XW/4720.

1999.   INCREASE IN TRAIN SERVICE BETWEEN KING'S CROSS AND CAMBRIDGE,
LETCHWORTH, HITCHIN AND WELWYN GARDEN CITY.

With reference to Minute No.1982; Submitted Memorandum, dated 16th March, by the Chief General Manager reporting that in consequence of road motor competition there has been a decrease in receipts from passenger traffic between Cambridge, Letchworth, Hitchin, Welwyn Garden City and London.

To meet the competition experienced between these points, two alternatives had been considered, viz:-

(1) The provision of 200 h.p. Sentinel Coaches of the articulated type.

(2) The use of ordinary trains of less than normal capacity, namely, an engine and three carriages.

For reasons stated in his Memorandum, the Chief General Manager recommended adoption of the second alternative, viz. that as from Monday 2nd May, 1932, the services between the towns mentioned be improved both in frequency and speed, particularly during the off peak periods.

As the traffic during these periods is not sufficiently large to warrant the employment of additional steam trains of normal capacity, it is proposed that 2 train sets consisting of engine, 3rd class carriage brake, Open 3rd class carriage, and Composite carriage, which are at present spare, be utilised to provide the increased services.

To improve the standard of comfort it is proposed that the coaches be fitted with arm rests in the 3rd class compartments and one end of the Open 3rd class carriage in each set converted into a Buffet Car to provide refreshment facilities on the trains.

The total cost of the work is estimated at £660, as under:-

	£
Fitting of arm rests	360
Conversion of Buffet Cars	300
	£660

The Committee recommended that authority be given for an expenditure of £660.

2.

FIG. 318   AUTHOR'S COLLECTION

168

At a Meeting of the LOCOMOTIVE COMMITTEE, held at

Marylebone Station, London, on Thursday, the 28th day of

April, 1932.

PRESENT:

A. K. McCOSH, ESQ.,   in the Chair.

William Whitelaw, Esq.,

The Rt. Hon. Lord Faringdon, C.H.,

W. B. Gair, Esq.,

The Rt. Hon. Viscount Grey of Fallodon, K.G.,

R. W. Matthews, Esq.,

W. K. Whigham, Esq.

Attended by:

        Sir Ralph Wedgwood,
        Mr. Newton,
        Mr. Gresley,
        Mr. Stamer,
        Mr. Richards,
        Mr. Groom,
        Mr. Dowsett, Assistant Secretary.

1493.   The Minutes of Meeting held on 17th March were read

and confirmed.

1494.   Statements were submitted as under:-

(a) Revenue Expenditure - Maintenance of Rolling Stock to
    26th March, 1932.
(b) Revenue Expenditure - Locomotive Running Expenses to
    26th March, 1932.
(c) Maintenance & Renewal of Rolling Stock - Statistical
    Return to 26th March, 1932.
(d) Engine Failures - Summary to 26th March, 1932.
(e) New Rolling Stock sent into Traffic. Position at
    26th March, 1932.
(f) New Works or Alterations of Works estimated to cost
    not more than £200 sanctioned during Quarter ended
    31st March, 1932, at an aggregate cost of £2,378.
    Expenditure of £2,378 APPROVED.
(g) Works in Progress sanctioned by Locomotive Committee
    estimated to cost over £1,000, 12 weeks to
    26th March, 1932.
(h) New Works Completed. Return of Savings realised,
    Quarter ended 31st March, 1932.
(i) Electrical Energy. Annual Costs, Year 1931.

1.

XW.4851

Brown Green

1496. WATER SOFTENING FOR LOCOMOTIVE BOILER PURPOSES.

Submitted Memorandum by the Chief Mechanical Engineer reporting the results of investigations made as to the quality of water supplies for locomotive boiler purposes in the various Sections, and as to the economies likely to be effected by the use of Water Softening Plants.

Special consideration had been given to water softening on the Main Line from King's Cross to Berwick and it is considered that greater economies would be secured by treating water on the Great Northern Section than on the North Eastern Section. It is therefore proposed that water softening plants be installed at Stations on the Great Northern Section as follows:-

Place.	Water to be softened in million gallons per annum.	Capital cost of Plant Installation etc. £.
King's Cross	220	11,330.
Hornsey and Ferme Park	83	4,592.
Langley	100	2,730.
Hitchin	99	2,979.
Offord	24	2,233.
New England	173	7,249.
Essendine	25	2,024.
Grantham	89.5	3,542.
Grantham Spittlegate	24.5	2,123.
Carried forward	838.	£38,802.

2.

FIG. 320   AUTHOR'S COLLECTION

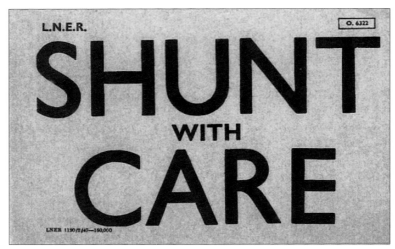

Wagon label (reduced size).

1496. Contd.	Place.	Water to be softened in million gallons per annum.	Capital cost of Plant Installation, etc.
			£.
	Brought forward -	838	38,802.
	Muskham	113	4,125.
	Retford	47	2,552.
	Scrooby and Doncaster	360	15,213.
		1,358.	£60,692.

the allocation of the expenditure being as under:-

	£.	£.
Purchase of Softening Plants		24,431.

Engineer's Department Work.

	£.	£.
Chemical Storage and Mixing Houses	2,440.	
Towers for Water Softeners	7,863.	
New Water Tanks	2,420.	
Piers for Tanks	3,173.	
New Water Mains	7,491.	
Sidings	1,060.	24,447.

Chief Mechanical Engineer's Work.

	£.	£.
Pumps, Boilers and Motors for Mixers	5,676.	
Sludge Removal Equipment	6,138.	11,814.
		£60,692.

L. & N. E. R.
SECRETARY'S OFFICE
APPROVED BY
WORKS COMMITTEE
28 APR 1932

It is estimated that an ultimate saving of £49,000 per annum will be realised in connection with Boiler Repairs and Renewals and Coal Consumption, and that after allowing for the annual cost of working the softening plants including Sinking Fund and repair charges, estimated at £24,467 per annum, a net saving of £24,533 per annum will be secured.

See Board
Minute No.
1457.

The Committee approved the proposals and recommended to the Board that the expenditure of £60,692 be authorised.

FIG. 321

AUTHOR'S COLLECTION

An engine shed plate originally fitted inside the cab (reduced size).

At a Meeting of the TRAFFIC COMMITTEE, held at Marylebone Station, London, on Thursday, the 2nd day of June, 1932.

PRESENT:

THE RT. HON. VISCOUNT GREY OF FALLODON, K.G., in the Chair.

William Whitelaw, Esq.,
The Rt. Hon. Lord Faringdon, C.H.,
H. T. Bailey, Esq.,
Sir Charles C. Barrie, M.P.,
Sir Charles A. Batho, Bart.,
O. R. H. Bury, Esq.,
The Hon. E. B. Butler-Henderson,
Major W. H. Carver, M.P.,
A. R. Gray, Esq.,
R. W. Matthews, Esq.,
Clarence D. Smith, Esq.,
Sir Murrough J. Wilson.

Attended by:

Sir Ralph Wedgwood,
Mr. Pritchard,
Mr. Calder,
Mr. Hornsby,
Mr. Thurston,
Mr. Oldham,
Mr. Barrington-Ward,
Mr. Marshall,
Mr. Mauldin,
Mr. Selway,
Mr. McLaren, Secretary.

2038.   Minutes of last Meeting (28th April) were read, confirmed and signed.

2039.   The following Returns were submitted:-

(a) Traffic Expenses, 4 weeks ended 23rd April, 1932.
(b) Revenue Returns, 4 weeks ended 23rd April, 1932.
(c) Running of Passenger Trains.
(d) Running of Freight Trains.
(e) Loaded Wagons Forwarded.
(f) Receipts and Expenditure in respect of Docks, Harbours and Wharves, 4 weeks ended 23rd April, 1932.

1.

FIG. 322   AUTHOR'S COLLECTION

XW.5261

2042. <u>POST OFFICE SORTING CARRIAGES</u>.

      Submitted Memorandum, dated 1st June, by the Chief General Manager reporting **that** following the accident at Charfield on the L.M.S. Line in October 1928, when a number of Post Office Sorters were injured through the wreckage taking fire, the Post Master General raised with the Railway Companies the question of the replacement of gas lighting by electric lighting apparatus in all Travelling Post Office Sorting Carriages.

      As a result of negotiations between the Railway Companies and the Post Office Authorities, the Railway Companies agreed to recommend to their respective Boards the conversion of suitable Post Office Sorting Carriages from gas to electric lighting on the basis that 75% of the cost would be borne by the Post Office, and the Post Office have agreed to contribute in this proportion.

      The present stock of L.N.E. Post Office Sorting Carriages is 26 made up as follows:-

<u>Electrically Lit</u>.

<u>No</u>.	<u>Type</u>.	<u>Age</u>.
3	Bogie	3 years.

<u>Gas Lit</u>.

6	Bogie	19-25 years.
7	Bogie	28-30 years.
10	Six-wheeled	30-47 years.
26		

      So far as the gas lit vehicles are concerned the matter has been investigated jointly with the Post Office Authorities and the following proposals agreed:-

	Total Cost.	Cost to Post Office.	Cost to L.N.E. Company.
	£	£	£
(1) To convert the 6 most modern <u>Bogie vehicles</u> to electric lighting, the Post Office to bear 75% of the cost	1,920	1,440	480

(**The 7** remaining Bogie Vehicles will have to be replaced within the next 5 years, and it is not proposed to convert them to electric lighting.)

3.

(Continued)

FIG. 323

AUTHOR'S COLLECTION

	Total Cost.	Cost to Post Office.	Cost to L.N.E. Co.
	£	£	£

2042.
Contd.

Brought forward — 1,920 / 1,440 / 480

(2) To withdraw the 10 six-wheeled
vehicles and replace these,
(together with two already withdrawn)
by 7 vehicles of modern type. The
Post Office have agreed to pay the
difference between the estimated
cost of replacing the 12 six-wheeled
vehicles by 12 others of similar
type (£12,800) and the total
estimated cost of the 7 new bogie
vehicles -(£18,530).
Difference - £5,730. — 18,530 / 5,730 / 12,800

(3) Certain minor additions and
improvements, such as electric
urns, cupboards, etc., have been
asked for by the Post Office,
affecting 13 vehicles, and the Post
Office will bear the whole cost
estimated at £572. — 572 / 572 / Nil.

Total — 21,022 / 7,742 / 13,280

The Committee recommended that authority be given for

a total expenditure of £21,022, the Post Office to bear

£7,742, and the L.N.E. proportion of the cost of the new

vehicles, viz. £12,800 - to be taken into account in

connection with the next Carriage Building Programme.

FIG. 324 AUTHOR'S COLLECTION

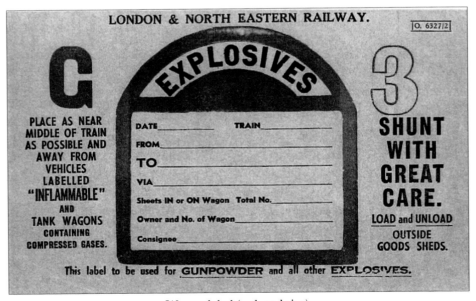

Wagon label (reduced size).

At a Meeting of the TRAFFIC COMMITTEE, held at Marylebone Station, London, on Thursday, the 24th day of November, 1932.

PRESENT:

THE RT. HON. VISCOUNT GREY OF FALLODON, K.G., in the Chair.

William Whitelaw, Esq.,

The Rt. Hon. Lord Faringdon, C.H.,

H. T. Bailey, Esq.,

Sir Charles C. Barrie, M.P.,

Sir Charles A. Batho, Bart.,

O. R. H. Bury, Esq.,

Major W. H. Carver, M.P.,

A. R. Gray, Esq.,

R. W. Matthews, Esq.,

Clarence D. Smith, Esq.,

F. L. Steel, Esq.,

Sir Murrough J. Wilson.

Attended by:

Mr. Calder,
Mr. Hornsby,
Mr. Thurston,
    Mr. Oldham,
    Mr. Brickwell,
    Mr. Marshall,
    Mr. Mauldin,
    Mr. Selway,
Mr. Gresley,
Mr. McLaren, Secretary.

2134.   Minutes of last Meeting (27th October) were read, confirmed and signed.

2135.   The following Returns were submitted :-

(a) Traffic Expenses, 4 weeks ended 8th October, 1932.
(b) Revenue Returns, 4 weeks ended 8th October, 1932.
(c) Running of Passenger Trains.
(d) Running of Freight Trains.
(e) Loaded Wagons Forwarded.
(f) Receipts and Expenditure in respect of Docks,
     Harbours and Wharves, 4 weeks ended 8th October, 1932.

1.

FIG. 325   AUTHOR'S COLLECTION

2136. <u>MINOR FACILITIES</u>:- <u>EAST COAST SERVICES</u>.

XW 3169   <u>WIRELESS RECEPTION</u>.

Submitted Memorandum, dated 23rd November, by
the Chief General Manager reporting on experiments, which
commenced in November 1930, with Wireless Reception on
certain train services, the expenditure thereon and receipts
therefrom.

The Chief General Manager, while of opinion that
it is reasonable to expect that the use of the facility
by the public will increase in future years so
as to shew a reasonable profit on the venture, does not
consider that the results as yet warrant further extension.
Meantime he proposed that the equipment in the train sets
already fitted be retained.

The expenditure on equipment and its installation
which amounts to £975 was primarily incurred as an item
of advertisement in the general popularisation of railway
services, but, in view of its permanent retention, the
Chief General Manager now recommended that the expenditure
be approved as an item of equipment.

XW.4483/1   <u>COCKTAIL BARS</u>.

With the commencement of the Summer Services
this year Cocktail Bars were introduced on the train sets
forming the Up and Down Non-Stop Flying Scotsman trains.
The Bars were constructed at one end of each of two
corridor third vehicles, at a total cost of £979, as under:-

In Company's Shops	£459
By Contractors	520
	£979

The net <u>profit</u> from the two Bars for the twelve
weeks 18th July to 8th October, 1932, amounted to £62,
as under:-

Receipts		£359
Expenses		297
	Profit	£ 62

2.

(Continued)

FIG. 326   AUTHOR'S COLLECTION

2136.
Contd.

The receipts in the Restaurant Cars on the "Flying Scotsman" trains for the 4 weeks ended October 8th, 1932, compared with the corresponding period of 1931, shew an increase, apart from the Cocktail Bars, so that the takings in these Bars may be regarded as new business.

As in the case of Wireless Reception, the expenditure on the Bars was primarily incurred as an item of advertisement, but since the measure of success obtained by the experiment warrants its retention, the Chief General Manager recommended that the expenditure be approved as an item of equipment of the train sets.

The Committee recommended that the total expenditure of £1,894 incurred on both facilities be confirmed as items of equipment of the train sets concerned.

FIG. 327   AUTHOR'S COLLECTION

A replica of the brass plaque affixed to *Mallard* to mark her world speed record.
The above, cast in aluminium, was one of a number cast and given to ex-LNER directors on the eve of nationalisation.
When *Mallard* was restored for display in the Clapham Railway Museum in 1963 the opportunity was taken
to sell copies of the plaque cast from the original – these can be recognised by the absence of metal
in the area just above where the stems of the laurel wreath cross.

XW. 6424

2146.   SCARBOROUGH-WHITBY-SALTBURN BRANCH:-   PURCHASE OF DIESEL
        RAIL COACH "TYNESIDE VENTURER".   (N. E. AREA)

With reference to Minute No.1934 recommending
an expenditure of £15,690 on three 200 H.P. Sentinel Steam
Coaches for working the Scarborough-Whitby-Saltburn Branch
and deferring for further consideration the question of the
provision of a fourth coach;   Submitted Memorandum, dated
24th November, by the Divisional General Manager (N.E.Area)
reporting that the Company have had on trial from
Sir W.G. Armstrong Whitworth & Co.(Engineers) Ltd., since
11th April, 1932, a 250 H.P. Diesel Electric Rail Coach
which has been employed on the Carlisle, North Wylam and
Consett Branches for six months, and recently transferred
to the Middlesbrough, Guisborough and Saltburn section
where it is still running.

During the whole of this period the coach has
worked efficiently and has not failed nor lost time owing
to mechanical troubles.

The travelling public prefer the Diesel to the
Sentinel steam coach, particularly, on account of the
absence of smoke, steam and flying sparks.

It is anticipated that the working cost of the
Diesel coach will be less than that of the 200 H.P.
Sentinel coach, particularly as regards fuel consumption.

The initial cost of the Diesel Coach is £9,343
as compared with a figure of £5,230 for a 200 H.P. Sentinel
Steam Coach, but it is considered that this extra cost will
be more than offset by the economy in working expenses.

The Committee recommended the purchase of the
Diesel Coach and referred the matter to the Locomotive
Committee.

12.

FIG. 328

AUTHOR'S COLLECTION

SPECIAL FITTINGS
applied to New England engines in December 1926

L O N D O N   &   N O R T H   E A S T E R N   R A I L W A Y
SPECIAL FITTINGS.   PETERBOROUGH DISTRICT. 1/12/26

Special fitting	Engines	Reference
Special Piston Iron Rings (L.H.)	4416	S.D.21/191.20.7.27
Piston Valve fitted with special release valve arrangement.	3457	22/9/16
Worthington-Simpson Pump	)Feed water 3476 Fitted 1922	Taken off May 1927
Dabeg Pump. Worked from crank & exhaust steam pumps water from tender into back.	)heater) 3500	-
Lockyer Improved Balanced Reg.	4002 & Pacifics	E.925B. 31/8/21
Davies & Metcalfe. New design of Auto. Valve for exhaust Injector.	4437 & all Darl. K.3. Class Engs.	P/1003. 9/3/23
Piston valves fitted with special pressure release valves.	4442.4422.4452.2551. 2552.	AWT.85 17/12/24
Tenders fitted with additional rail for heavy mileage turns.	4413	-
Super-unit Elements.	3594	A.924. 7/5/23
Cast steel piston heads 1/2" less than diameter of cylr. etc.	3465. 3468	AWT.156.17/3/25
Trial Super.Tubes with Copper Ends.	4443	E/1076. 2/4/25
Alteration to Valve Lubricator.	2557	LRG/E1433.8/4/25
G.C.Type of Eccentric strap liner with enlarged oil cup. (attention to be called if extension pieces work loose).	3256. 3987. 4408	AWT.19. 20/4/25
New type of Grease Separator.	3285.4421.4405.4443	AWT.68. 23/4/25
Solid copper joints for Supr. elements.	3571	AWT.107.15/1/25
H56.type Springs J.50.Class Engs.	3221	AWT.81. 7/7/26
Lubrication of Horn Cheeks.	2548	AWT.97. 7/7/26
Piston Valves with Narrow rings.	2548.4476.4480.2550	AWT.21. 7/7/26
Ring spring buffers & drawgear	118. 2547	AWT.192. 7/7/26
Steam Pipe Joints. "Walkerite" "GOLDEN"	4445.3289.3291.2548. 4479.2549.109.4406.4476. 4429.3285.3286.3294.4438. 4446.4480.4410.2550.2556. 2557.2561.3283.3290.2551. 3494.2558.3296.4401.4407. 4430.4439.4448.112.	AWT.86a 6/7/26

FIG. 329

AUTHOR'S COLLECTION

LONDON & NORTH EASTERN RAILWAY

SPECIAL FITTINGS.   PETERBOROUGH DISTRICT. 1/12/26

Special fitting	Engines	Reference
Large Flue Tube screwed into Tubeplate.	6264.6504.6541	AWT.2. 6/7/26
Oil resistance hose to axleboxes.	2556.2558.2559.2561. 2548.4476.4480.2550. 2551.3255.2547.112.	AWT.97ab.1/7/26
Bosch Lubricator.	3462	AWT.137.6/10/24
Special "S" Piston Heads.	3546.3548.3597.	AWT.156.27/4/25
Mech.Lubr.gearing J.6Class Engs. strengthened type of gearing.	3599	AWT.157.29/6/26
Piston Tail Rods.	3465. 3468.	AWT.156. 9/7/25
Valve Spindle Crosshead Cotters.	3488.3490.3492.2547. 4471.4475.2543.	AWT.158.26/3/26
"Victor" packing for Superheated steam.	3440.3594.4431.4439.	AWT.8. 30/12/25
Brick Arches. - Low Camber.	2547	LRG/E.3057.8/4/26
Eccentric Ribbed Piston Valve Rings.	3500	AWT.178.30/7/25
Big End Bolts made of nickel steel stamped "N".	3837.4522.4504.3555.	AWT.76a.21/5/25
Broad Ring Piston Valves with eccentric ribs.	3488. 3489.	AWT.178.16/3/26
Axlebox Lubrication Flexible Armoured rubber feeds.	4479	AWT.105. 7/9/25
Collins Improved Firebars.	3478	AWT.172.28/10/25
Special lubricating gearing strengthened pattern.	2548	AWT.57. 7/7/26
Steam Pipe Joints. Lens shaped rings.	4414. 3293	AWT.86. 28/7/26
Brake Shaft Safety Stays.	3255.3259.3283.3285. 3286.3296.4430.3282. 4406.3290.4410.3283. 4429.4438.4445.	AWT.106.11/8/26
Cyl.relief valves 2.6.0 engs. built at Darlington.	75.80.109.111.118. 121.126.134.140.141 146.153.167.203.	AWT.126. 2/9/26
Steam Pipe Joints Armoured. "Walkerite"	3294	AWT.86a.22/9/26

FIG. 330

AUTHOR'S COLLECTION

L O N D O N & N O R T H E A S T E R N R A I L W A Y

SPECIAL FITTINGS.   PETERBOROUGH DISTRICT. 1/12/26

Special fitting	Engines	Reference
New type of Packing (C.I) to Piston Rods.	3283	AWT.8. 5/10/26
Cross stay on Atlantic engines with running shaft brackets.	3289.3291.3294.4401. 4407.4414.4439.4448.	LRG/E.6135.7.7.26
Big End Brasses K.1. & K.2. Engs.	4640. 4641.	15.6.25
Pacific Engines fitted with broached pistons.	2547. 2558. 2561.	AWT.201.27.11.26
.C. Type Combined Piston & Pressure release valve.	2551	AWT.21.27.11.26
Felt Oiling Pads (G.E.R. type)	2556.2557.2561.4476.	AWT.105 11/1/27
Franklyn Grease Lubrication	4673	AWT.210 30/12/26
Cast Iron Piston Packing	3285	AWT.8 23/12/26

FIG. 331

AUTHOR'S COLLECTION

ENGINE CHIMNEY DRAWINGS
LNER notation used throughout with 1924 numbering of engines

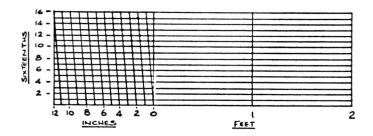

READING DIAGONAL SCALE

ALL DIMENSIONS MEASURED HORIZONTALLY

ALL DIMENSIONS TO BE TAKEN

ON BASE LINE OF SCALE

For example:

1'-0" is to right of zero up to 1 ft. mark on scale

1'-6" is to right of zero up to 1 ft. mark on scale plus 6 in. to left of zero

1'-6⅜" is to right of zero up to 1 ft. mark on scale plus 6 in. to left of zero plus up the diagonal line ⁶/₁₆ in. i.e. ⅜ in.

ALL CHIMNEY DRAWINGS SCALED

APPROXIMATELY AT 1 in. = 1 ft.

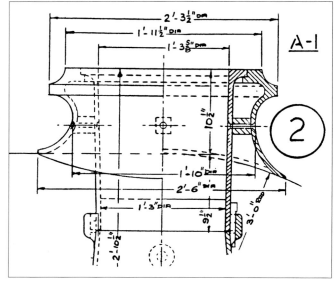

FIG. 333. 4-6-2 Type A-1 class engines. Fitted to 4481 only, E.O. 297. Reference drg. I-308N. Pattern Nos. Chimney 27992, Liner 27837, Cowl 1459.

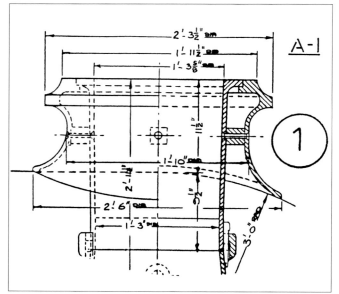

FIG. 332. 4-6-2 Type A-1 class engines. Fitted to 4470 to 4480 built 1922-23 E.O. 293 4470/1, E.O. 297 4472/80, Reference drg I-278N. Pattern Nos. Chimney 27362, Liner 27363, Cowl 1459.

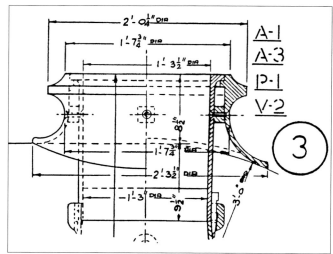

FIG. 334. 4-6-2 Type A-1 and A-3 class engines. Fitted to all engines built after 1923. 2-8-2 Type P-1 class engines Nos. 2393 and 2394, E.O. 303. 2-6-2 Type V-2 class engines. Reference drg. I-768 liner and chimney; I-766 cowl. Pattern Nos. Chimney 28290, Liner 28297, Cowl 1459. Reference drg nos. and pattern nos. refer to Class A-1, A-3, P-1 and V-2.

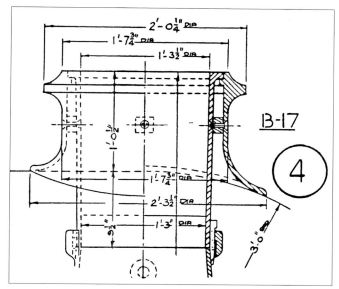

FIG. 335. 4-6-0 Type B-17 class engines. Reference drg I-768 liner and chimney; I-766 cowl. Pattern Nos. Chimney not known; Liner not known; Cowl 1459.

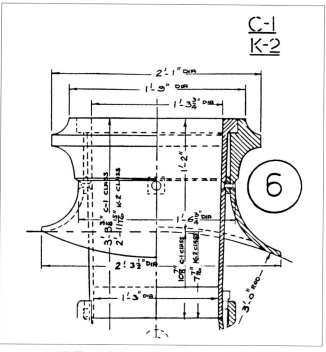

FIG. 337. 4-4-2 Type C-1 class engines. Altered to suit N.B. and G.E. section. Loading gauge fitted to engines 4447 and 4419. Pattern Nos. Chimney 27921, Liner 34602, Cowl 1459. 2-6-0 Type K-2 class engines. Reference drg I-300 liner and chimney; I-766 cowl. Pattern Nos. Chimney 27921, Liner 34602, Cowl 1459. Altered to suit N.B. and G.E. Section loading gauge.

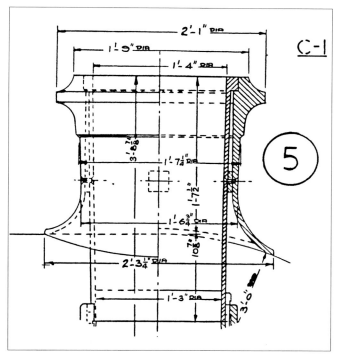

FIG. 336. 4-4-2 Type C-1 class engines. Reference drg I-83 liner and chimney; I-766 cowl. Pattern Nos. Chimney 1075, Liner 1400, Cowl 1459.

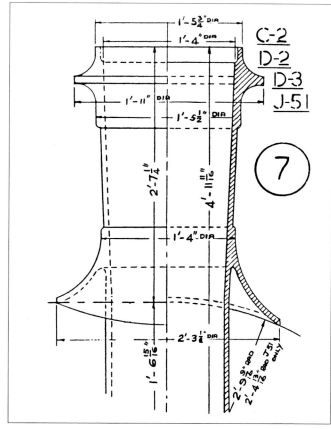

FIG. 338 (right). 4-4-2 Type C-2 class engines. Reference drg I-125N. For superheater fitted engines C-2 class (see drg I-238N altered cowl fastening). 4-4-0 Type D-2 class engines. Reference drg I-125N. For superheated fitted engines D-2 class (see drg I-238N altered cowl fastening). 4-4-0 Type D-2 class engines. Reference drg I-125N. 0-6-0 Type J-51 class engines. Reference drg I-125N. Pattern Nos. Chimney 12785, Liner –, Cowl 12784 (C-2, D-2 and D-3 class engines); Chimney 12785, Cowl 23188 (fitted to J-51 class engines).

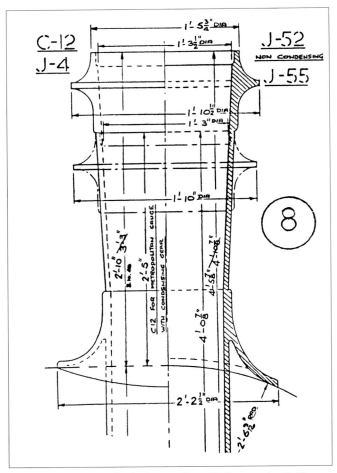

FIG. 339. 4-4-2 Type C-12 class engines. Reference drg I-48 non-condensing; I-58 condensing. Chain dotted lines show shortened chimney fitted to C-12 class engines built to Metropolitan loading gauge. Pattern No. 12788 condensing. 0-6-0 Type J-4 class engines. Reference drg I-827. Cast iron pattern used for base 0-6-0 type J-52 class engines. Reference drg I-827 non-condensing. Cast iron pattern used for base. 0-6-0 Type J-55 class engines. Reference drg I-827. Cast iron pattern used for base.

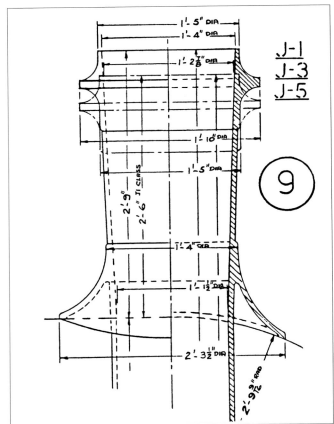

FIG. 340. 0-6-0 Type J-1 class engines. Chain dotted lines show shortened chimney for J-1 class engines. Reference drg I-109N. Pattern Nos. Chimney 20427, Cowl 12784. 0-6-0 Type J-3 class engines. Reference drg I-109N. Pattern Nos. Chimney 21345, Cowl 12784. 0-6-0 Type J-5 class engines. Reference drg I-109N. Pattern Nos. Chimney 21345, Cowl 12784. Note! 4-4-2 Type C-2 class engine. Reference drg I-109N. Fitted to engine No. 3271 only. Pattern Nos. Chimney 20427, Cowl 12784.

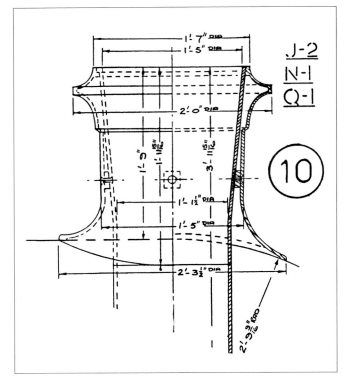

FIG. 341 (right). 0-6-0 Type J-2 class engines. Reference drg I-102N for chimney and liner. For cowl and fastening see drg I-238 3/10/40. Pattern Nos. Chimney 19861, Liner 10035, Cowl 25151. 0-6-2 Type N-1 class engines. Reference drg I-102N for chimney and liner. For cowl and fastening see drg I-238 3/10/40. Pattern Nos. Chimney 19861, Liner 10035, Cowl 25151. 0-8-0 Type Q-1 class engines. Reference drg I-102N for chimney and liner. For cowl and fastening see drg I-125 4/7/42. Pattern Nos. Chimney 19861, Liner 10035, Cowl 12784.

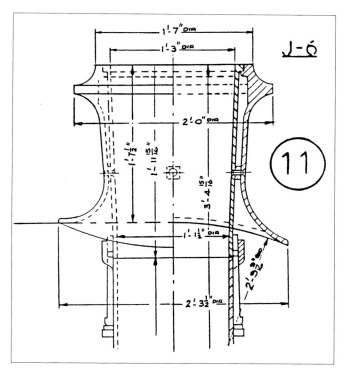

FIG. 342. 0-6-0 Type J-6 class engines. Reference drg I-774 chimney and liner; I-238 cowl. Pattern Nos. Chimney 34482, Liner 34483, Cowl 25151. Final chimney type fitted to suit LNER loading gauge 6/39 to 6/43.

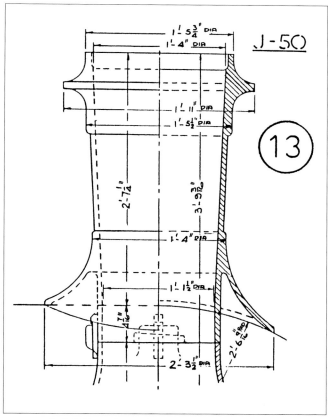

FIG. 344. 0-6-0 Type J-50 class engines. Reference drg I-729 chimney; I-125 cowl for engines built before 1937. Reference drg I-729 chimney and cowl for engines built after 1937. (N.B. First batch built 3221-3330 were fitted with wide tapering chimneys [not drawn].) Pattern Nos. Chimney 12785, Liner –, Cowl 12704, Cowl 1937 onwards 23188.

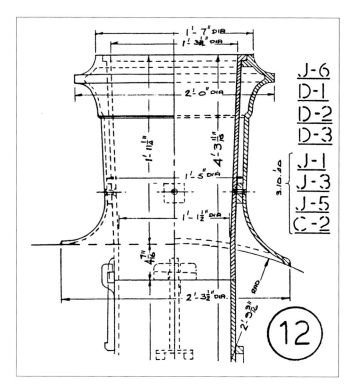

FIG. 343 (left). 4-4-0 Type D-1 class engines. Reference drg I-238N. Altered to suit N.B. section loading gauge. 12/24. Pattern Nos. Chimney 23164, Liner 25462, Cowl 25151. 4-4-0 Type D-2 class engines. Reference drg I-238N. Altered to suit G.E. section loading gauge. Final type of chimney from 3/39. Pattern Nos. Chimney 23164, Liner 25462, Cowl 25151. 4-4-0 Type D-3 class engines. Reference drg I-238N. Altered to suit G.E. section loading gauge. Final type of chimney from 3/39. 0-6-0 Type J-1 class engines. Reference drg I-238N. Final type of chimney. (N.B. some engines finished their life with turned down tall chimneys, i.e. 2'-6" high with 1½" turned off upper lip. This modification done during the 1930s. Pattern Nos. Chimney 23164, Liner 25462, Cowl 25151. 0-6-0 Type J-3 class engines. Reference drg I-238N. Final type of chimney. Pattern Nos. Chimney 23164, Liner 25062, Cowl 25151. 0-6-0 Type J-5 class engines. Reference drg I-238N. Final type of chimney fitted to suit LNER loading gauge. 4-4-2 Type C-2 class engines. Reference drg I-238N. (N.B. No evidence exists that this chimney was ever fitted to any member of the class.) Pattern Nos. Chimney 23164, Liner 25462, Cowl 25151.

2'-11½" high chimneys fitted when rebuilt from J-53 to keep within Metropolitan loading gauge. Subsequently reduced to 2'-10" high which was then considered standard for condensing engines. Pattern No. Chimney 21750.

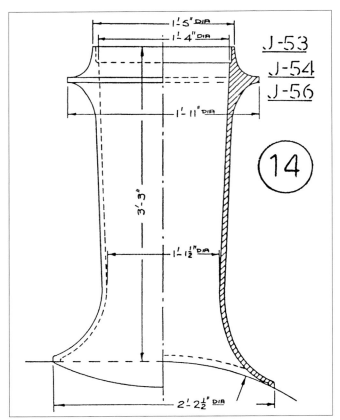

FIG. 345. 0-6-0 Type J-53 class engines. Cast iron pattern without number. Much boiler change. Smoke box radius depended on boiler diameter. 0-6-0 Type J-54 class engines. Cast iron pattern without number. Much boiler change. Smoke box radius depended on boiler diameter. 0-6-0 J-56 class engines. Cast iron pattern without number. Much boiler change. Smoke box radius depended on boiler diameter.

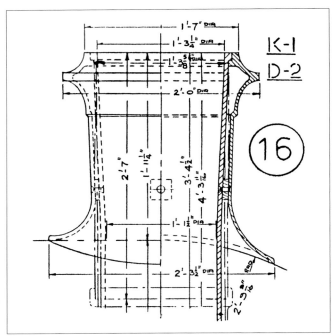

FIG. 347. 2-6-0 Type K-1 class engines. Reference drg I-165N. Pattern Nos. Chimney 23164, Liner 23165, Cowl 23188 (for 4630 engine E.O. 270); Chimney 23164, Liner 23696, Cowl 23697 (for 4631-38 engines E.O. 272). (N.B. See drg 17 for engines reduced to suit G.E. and N.B. loading gauge. 4-4-0 Type D-2 class engines. Reference drg I-165N. Pattern No. Chimney 23164, Liner 23696, Cowl 12784. Altered to suit G.E. and N.B. loading gauge.

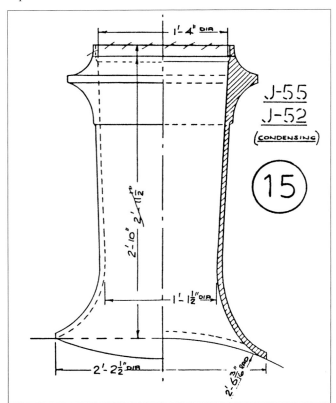

FIG. 346. 0-6-0 Type J-55 class engines. Final chimney fitted. Pattern No. Chimney 21750. 0-6-0 Type J-52 class engines

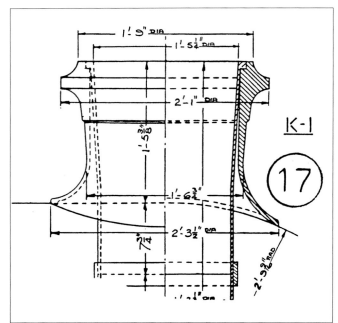

FIG. 348. 2-6-0 Type K-1 class engines. Reference drg I-174N. Pattern Nos. Chimney 219, Liner (new mild steel liner), Cowl 23697. Altered to suit G.E. and N.B. loading gauge. Originally fitted to 0-8-2 type tank engines built to suit Metropolitan loading gauge.

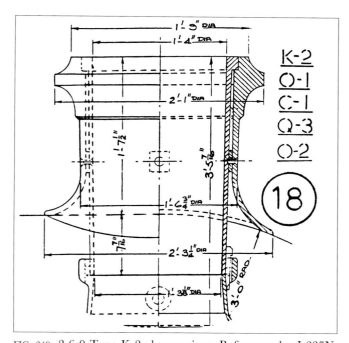

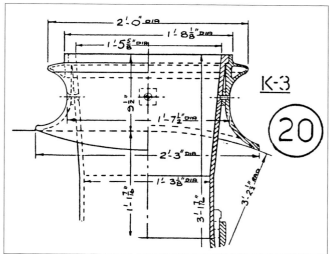

FIG. 349. 2-6-0 Type K-2 class engines. Reference drg I-237N. Pattern Nos. Chimney 1075, Liner 23989, Cowl 1459. For engines altered to suit G.E. and N.B. loading gauge see drg 6. 2-8-0 Type O-1 class engines. Reference drg I-237N. Pattern Nos. Chimney 1075, Liner 23989, Cowl 1459. Reclassified O-3 2/1944. Originally fitted to engine Nos. 3456-60 and 3462-76. New fitting from 1940 (drg No. 27). 4-4-2 Type C-1 class engine. Reference drg I-237N. Fitted to engine No. 3279. (N.B. Major difference being height of top of chimney to base of cowl. Chimney height reduced to 1'-4" upon rebuild to two cylinder 4/38 [see drg 27]. Changed again to standard C-1 chimney to cowl layout 4/46.) Pattern Nos. Chimney 1075, Liner 23989, Cowl 1459. 0-8-0 Type Q3 class engine. Reference drg I-237N. Fitted to engine No. 3420. Pattern Nos. Chimney 1075, Liner 23989, Cowl 1459. 2-8-0 Type O-2 class engines. Reference drg I-237N. Pattern Nos. Chimney 1075, Liner 23989, Cowl 1459. Originally fitted to engine Nos. 3461, 3477-86. Rebuilt with chimney drg No. 27 in 1940 to confirm to LNER composite loading gauge. This brought Type O-2 into line with 1923/4 build which already had drg No. 27 chimney – viz Type 02/2 3487-3501, 02/3 2954-61. Chimney drg No. 27 also fitted to Gresley rebuild 04/5 ex G.C.

FIG. 351. 2-6-0 Type K-3 class engines. Reference drg 10728D. 17 series engines built at Darlington. 50 engines ordered October 1923. Engine Nos. between 17 and 200 filling vacant spaces. No pattern quoted for chimney and liner, but cowl was 1459.

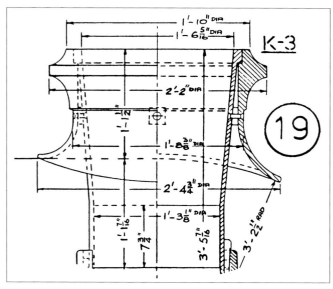

FIG. 350. 2-6-0 Type K-3 class engines. Reference drg I-260N. Fitted to engine Nos. 4000-4009. Pattern Nos. Chimney 26480, Liner 26111, Cowl 1459.

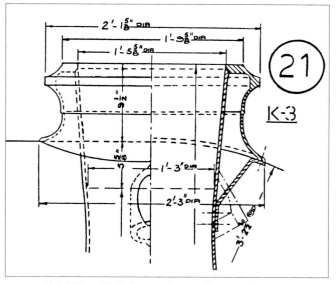

FIG. 352. 2-6-0 Type K-3 class engines. Reference drg I-371N. 1300 series engines built at Doncaster. 20 engines ordered August 1927. Engine Nos. between 1300 and 98 filling vacant spaces. Pattern Nos. Chimney 30503, Liner 30575, Cowl not required.

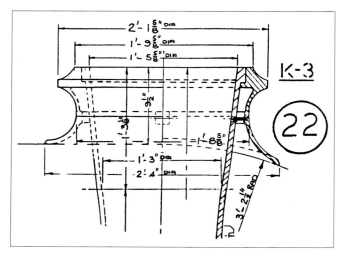

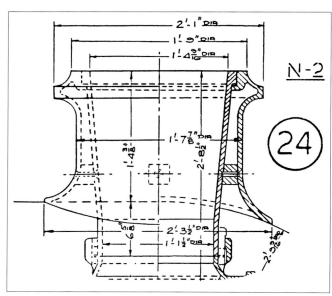

FIG. 353. 2-6-0 Type K-3 class engines. Reference drg I-612. Later series built at Darlington. 9 engines ordered December 1928. Engine Nos. 2761-2769. Pattern Nos. Chimney 33665, Liner 33666, Cowl 33667. (N.B. Notes concerning all K-3 class engines – i.e. drgs 19, 20, 21 and 22 – by approximately June 1941 all had chimney drg 22 to confirm to LNER composite loading gauge – i.e. 2'-4" base diameter. This included rebuild K-5 engine No. 206.

FIG. 355. 0-6-2 Type N-2 class engines. Reference drg I-323N. Non-condenser fitted. Pattern Nos. Chimney 28959, Liner 28958, Cowl 23188.

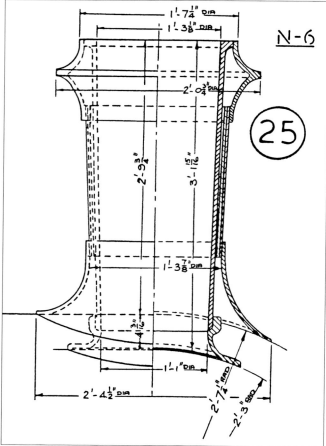

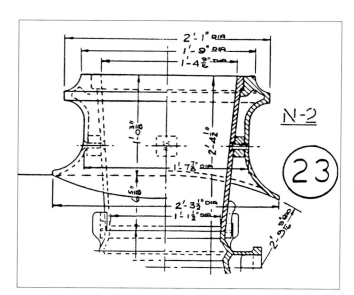

FIG. 354. 0-6-2 Type N-2 class engines. Reference drg I-265N. Fitted with condensers for Metropolitan service. Pattern Nos. Chimney 26641, Liner 26642, Cowl 23188.

FIG. 356. 0-6-2 Type N-6 class engines. Reference drg TX-161. Replacement for Robinson chimney. Fitting started from September 1931.

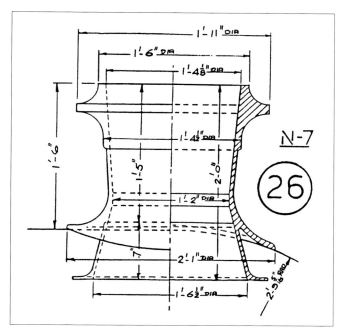

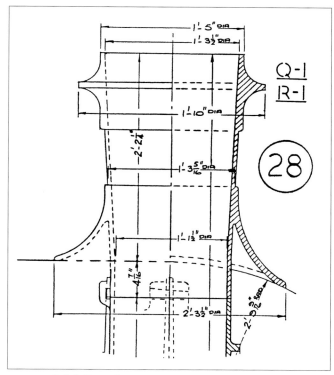

FIG. 357. 0-6-2 Type N-7 class engines. Reference drg N-7-28N. Doncaster built series E.O. 310 to 313. Engine Nos. 2600-31. 1927-28 build. Pattern Nos. Chimney 29746, Cowl 29811.

FIG. 359. 0-8-2 Type R-1 class engines. Reference drg I-101N. Pattern Nos. Chimney 12788, Cowl 25151, Cowl 12784 for non-superheater engines. 0-8-0 Type Q1 class engines. Reference drg I-101N. Pattern Nos. Chimney 12788, Cowl 25151, Cowl 12784 for non-superheater engines.

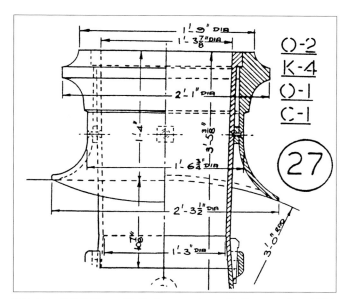

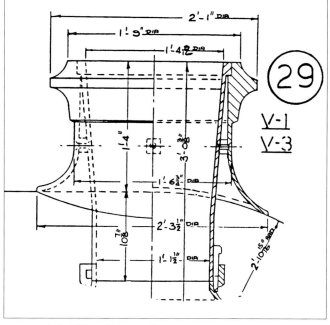

FIG. 358. 2-8-0 Type O-2 class engines. Reference drg I-311 liner and chimney; I-766 cowl. As rrebuilt from 12/1938 O2/2 class engines. From O-2 class engines Nos. 3487-96 E.O. 298, 3497-501 E.O. 299. Built 1923/4. (N.B. Original chimney, etc. [see drg 18]). Engine Nos. 3461 also O2/1 Nos. 3477-86. Reference drg I-254N [not drawn]. Pattern Nos. Chimney 1075, Liner 26111, Cowl 1459. Major differences inside diameter of chimney 1'-6⁵⁄₁₆", height of chimney 1'-7½". All other dimensions as shown on drg 18. 2-8-0 Type O-1 class engines. Reference drg I-311 liner and chimney; I-766 cowl. Pattern Nos. Chimney 28036, Liner 28037, Cowl 1459. New fitting from 1940, previously original chimney, etc. [see drg 18]. Engine Nos. 3456-60 and 3462-76. 2-6-0 Type K-4 class engines. Reference drg I-311 liner and chimney; I-766 cowl. Pattern Nos. Chimney 28036, Liner 28037, Cowl 1459. 4-4-2 Type C-1 class engine. Reference drg I-311 liner and chimney; I-766 cowl. Pattern Nos. Chimney 28036, Liner 28037, Cowl 1459. Chimney reduced to 1'-4" high upon rebuild to 2 cylinder. Changed again to standard C-1 chimney 4/46 [drg No. 5]. (N.B. Chimney drg 27 used by Thompson on engine Type B-1, K-1, K1/1 (rebuilt K4) and L-1.

FIG. 360. 2-6-2 Type V-1 and V-3 class engines. Reference drg I-390. Pattern Nos. Chimney 28036 altered base, Liner 31241, Cowl 23188.

BIBLIOGRAPHY
and further suitable reading covering the LNER

A Gresley Anthology, edited by Geoffrey Hughes, Wild Swan (1994).

A Pictorial History of LNER Wagons, Peter Tatlow, Oxford Publishing Co. (1976).

A Pictorial Record of LNER Constituent Signalling, A. A. Maclean, Oxford Publishing Co. (1983).

Bill Hoole, Engineman Extraordinary, P. W. B. Semmens, Ian Allan Ltd (1966).

East Coast from King's Cross, Eric Neve, Ian Allan Ltd (1983).

East Coast Pacifics at Work, P. N. Townend, Ian Allan Ltd (1982).

Enginemen Elite, Norman McKillup, Ian Allan Ltd (1958).

Gresley Locomotives: A Pictorial History, B. Haresnape, Ian Allan Ltd (1981).

Gresley Pacifics, Cecil J. Allen, Ian Allan Ltd (1950).

Gresley's Coaches, Coaches built for the GNR, ECJS & LNER 1905-1953, Michael Harris, David & Charles (1973).

LNER Album, Vol. 1, Brian Stephenson, Ian Allan Ltd (1970).

LNER Album, Vol. 2, Brian Stephenson, Ian Allan Ltd (1970).

LNER Reflections, edited by Nigel Harris, Silver Link Publishing (1985).

LNER Sheds in Camera, John Hooper, Oxford Publishing Co. (1984).

LNER Standard & Gresley Carriages, Michael Harris, published by Mallard Books (1998).

LNER, Geoffrey Hughes, Ian Allan Ltd (1986).

Locomotives of Sir Nigel Gresley, O. S. Nock, The Railway Publishing Co. Ltd (1945).

Locomotives of the LNER, RCTS (1963-1994). 19 volumes covering the different classes, each obtainable separately. Regarded as the definitive work on LNER locomotive history.

Motive Power Chief Vol. 2, A. J. Somers, XPRESS Publishing (1997).

Nigel Gresley, Locomotive Engineer, F. A. S. Brown, Ian Allan Ltd (1961).

Profile of the A4s, Whiteley & Morrison, Oxford Publishing Co. (1985).

The Great British Railway Station 'King's Cross', Chris Hawkins, Irwell Press (1990).

The Gresley Legacy, Martin Smith, Argus Books (1992).

The Power of the A1s, A2s and A3s, Whiteley & Morrison, Oxford Publishing Co. (1982).

The Power of the A4s, Brian Morrison, Oxford Publishing Co. (1978).

The Power of the B17s and B2s, Peter Swinger, Oxford Publishing Co. (1988).

Top Shed, P. N. Townend, Ian Allan Ltd (1975).

Triumph and Beyond, The East Coast Main Line 1939-1959, B. W. L. Brooksbank, Challenger Publications (1997).

Yeadons Register of LNER Locomotives
Vols 1-6, Irwell Press.
Vols 7-13, Challenger Publications.
Vols 14 onward, Challenger UK/ Booklaw Railbus.

A number of these books, some of which were consulted in the preparation of this book, are out of print, and in such cases it may be possible to find remaining copies in specialist bookshops.

INDEX